# SHADOW CELL

# SHADOW CELL

## AN INSIDER ACCOUNT OF AMERICA'S NEW SPY WAR

# ANDREW BUSTAMANTE
# & JIHI BUSTAMANTE

LB

Little, Brown and Company

*New York   Boston   London*

Copyright © 2025 by Andrew Bustamante and Jihi Bustamante

Hachette Book Group supports the right to free expression and the value of copyright. The purpose of copyright is to encourage writers and artists to produce the creative works that enrich our culture.

The scanning, uploading, and distribution of this book without permission is a theft of the authors' intellectual property. If you would like permission to use material from the book (other than for review purposes), please contact permissions@hbgusa.com. Thank you for your support of the authors' rights.

Little, Brown and Company
Hachette Book Group
1290 Avenue of the Americas, New York, NY 10104
littlebrown.com

First Edition: September 2025

Little, Brown and Company is a division of Hachette Book Group, Inc. The Little, Brown name and logo are trademarks of Hachette Book Group, Inc.

The publisher is not responsible for websites (or their content) that are not owned by the publisher.

The Hachette Speakers Bureau provides a wide range of authors for speaking events. To find out more, go to hachettespeakersbureau.com or email hachettespeakers@hbgusa.com.

Little, Brown and Company books may be purchased in bulk for business, educational, or promotional use. For information, please contact your local bookseller or the Hachette Book Group Special Markets Department at special.markets@hbgusa.com.

ISBN 9780316572149

Book interior design by Marie Mundaca

LCCN is available at the Library of Congress.

Printing 1, 2025

LSC-C

Printed in the United States of America

*To Sina and Alai, our greatest inspiration and our most rewarding mission. Mommy and Daddy love you.*

# CONTENTS

# AUTHORS' NOTE

The story you are about to read is real. One of the most modern and detailed CIA memoirs in print, this book has taken more than three years to meet CIA's rigorous operational review process. As authors, we are committed to advancing the public's understanding of, and appreciation for, professional intelligence operations and the incredible men and women who fight America's spy war every day. As former CIA officers, we are unwavering in our commitment to protect America's national security secrets and combat those adversaries who would try to use our memoir against the country we love. It is precisely because of these two commitments that we worked so diligently (and for so long) with CIA to bring you this story.

For this reason, too, we can't tell you the real name of the country that we refer to in this book as Falcon. But we *can* tell you that it's a place with centuries of history, a vibrant culture, a wonderful people…and a government implacably opposed to the United States and its allies.

When we showed CIA an early version of the story we intended to tell in this book, the Agency informed us that it considers the name of this country—along with other details that could be used to identify it—to be classified information. After much discussion, we agreed to coin the name Falcon for our target country, along with pseudonyms for other persons and places in our story, among them the name of a mole who penetrated CIA. We have made other changes to the mole's identifying features, and these obfuscations seem fitting, in a way, as he was not unmasked until long after we left CIA—meaning that his identity was a mystery to us, too, during the time frame that we cover in this book.

In addition, we have changed certain other details in our narrative. It goes without saying that we have changed the true names of our CIA colleagues and their sources. By extension, we have altered superficial details that might be used to identify them, such as personal descriptors and the exact timing of events. We have also avoided describing certain techniques and technologies that are essential to modern-day CIA operations—but with no adverse effect on the basic story that we're telling in this book, which at its core is a tale of human intelligence, not gadgets and gizmos. All dialogue has been reconstructed.

Despite these precautions, the heart of our account remains very much intact, and its deeper meaning shines through. *Shadow Cell* shows how a small band of misfits came together to take on the colossus of Falcon intelligence, and how in the process they wound up changing how CIA operates. But even more fundamentally, our story is a love letter to the courageous men and women who serve in the ranks of CIA. It is about an outstanding team that did outstanding work at a time when America needed outstanding bravery. The only reason we are the ones telling this story is that we eventually left CIA. As far as we know, every other member of the Cell is still on the inside. They are the real heroes, and this book is dedicated to them. Without their efforts and sacrifices, the world would be a much more dangerous place.

# SHADOW CELL

# PROLOGUE

## ANDY

It was snowing that morning, and the snow was gray. Car exhaust, a feature of Kestrel, the Falcon capital, had turned it the color of pixels on a closed-circuit monitor. As I watched the scene through the lobby's big glass doors, I realized something. For the first time on any of my trips inside Falcon, I was not being followed.

On a normal day, I would be observed from the moment I set foot in the hotel lobby. The elevator doors would open and there would be my minder, furtively eyeing me over a newspaper and a cup of hot coffee. When I left for the day, he — it was always a man — would tail me out of the hotel, and the dance would begin. With the minder at my back, I would do my best to seem as innocent as possible: I would go clothes shopping, eat a big breakfast, take long walks through quiet little parks. Eventually, the minder would get bored and wander off to look for a more interesting target. Then I could start doing real espionage.

But on that snowy morning, nobody was watching me at all. I wandered around the lobby just to be sure. None of the patrons or staff so much as glanced my way. At long last, it seemed, I had reached

3

intelligence nirvana. I had blended in so effectively that I was completely invisible.

This was the culmination of everything that I had been working on for the past year alongside Jihi, my wife and partner in espionage. Called upon to help build CIA's new network of sources inside Falcon, we created a whole new way of doing business. The Cell, as we will call it, was based on—of all things—the modus operandi of al-Qaeda, a terrorist network that America had been battling since before 9/11. Like that organization, the Cell was built on maintaining utmost secrecy, even from most of our colleagues within the Agency itself. And to judge by the complete absence of any surveillance directed at us, it was working.

A surge of excitement ran through my body. Now was the time to attempt the sorts of covert actions that no intelligence officer can pull off while under surveillance: for instance, case potential meeting locations with sources, dead drop items for retrieval later, and purchase materials for future operations. I could do it all, and no one would even know I was here.

I strode out the glass doors, eager to start my mission. Almost immediately, the acrid smell of exhaust engulfed me—and with it, a queasy feeling of a different kind.

What had I been thinking? *This was Falcon.* The intelligence services here were among the most capable in the world. They were patient, brutal, and above all: *paranoid*. If I felt invisible, it was because they *wanted* me to feel that way.

Now that I thought about it, wasn't there a better explanation for the absence of eyes on me? I didn't see anyone because the team watching me now was better trained, better equipped, and capable of staying hidden in the shadows. Despite the bitter cold, I began to sweat. My vision swam. My coat seemed to weigh me down like a diving bell. My case wasn't being ignored; it was being escalated. And that meant…

*They were coming for me.*

## JIHI

About eighteen months before Andy's fateful mission into Kestrel, Falcon opened a new front in its secret war with the United States. Classified reports from foreign intel partners painted a grim but clear picture—Falcon was working hard to penetrate American media, industry, and even our professional intel services. A mole had penetrated one of Langley's most elite and sensitive divisions, known internally as Falcon House. The identity of this mole would remain a mystery for nearly a decade.

America was losing ground all over the globe even as Falcon was boosting its military, developing advanced weaponry, deepening relations with other US adversaries, redoubling cyberattacks, and preparing to invade its neighbors. With America unable to predict Falcon's moves, the US and its personnel overseas were thrust into the crosshairs.

Desperate to build upon its existing intelligence network, CIA's Falcon House did something unprecedented: it looked beyond its own walls and turned to new recruits. Andy and I were tapped to lead the effort: two newlyweds, just twenty-nine years old, with zero experience operating against Falcon. We would need all the help we could get—and all the luck.

It was a race against time: we had to build a new intelligence network before the mole could unmask us and tear everything down. CIA wanted us to try something different. They would get their wish, though perhaps not in quite the ways they expected.

Against all odds, the new model we created—which many initially dismissed as crazy—would go on to transform the way America gathers intelligence.

This book is the story of how we did it.

# PART I
# SLIDING DOORS

## SCIMITAR

Call him Scimitar. He had given his entire adult life in service to the United States. He had enlisted in the US Army as an eighteen-year-old kid out of the Midwest, at the tail end of the Cold War. Then he joined CIA. The Agency must have seen potential in Scimitar, because they made him a case officer—one of the elite corps of clandestine agents trusted with meeting hostile human sources face-to-face and learning their secrets. To boot, Scimitar was assigned to spy on one of America's most dangerous adversaries, Falcon.

Now, in middle age, what did Scimitar have to show for it? He had been passed over for promotion after promotion. He had watched lesser officers snag all the best assignments. He had been denied proper credit for his achievements. Scimitar had risked his life for...what, exactly? Soon enough, his two sons—twins from a previous marriage—would be heading to college. They deserved the best, but on a government salary, that might not be possible. Scimitar's relationship with their mother had fallen apart under the weight of secrecy that comes with an intelligence career—a common story among Agency officers. His second wife, younger than the first, was far from eager to spend so much on these boys she barely knew. In short, Scimitar needed to up his earnings.

For all these reasons, Scimitar wanted out. He had a plan. A former colleague from the Agency had built a successful career on the outside running fraud investigations for a big global bank. When Scimitar mentioned his long experience spying on Falcon—where the bank, like many companies, was looking to expand—he was hired. Just like that, he was on his way—out of the Agency, out of the United States, toward a better salary, a corner office, a better life for his sons.

Before too long, however, Scimitar was going to discover the downside of working in the private sector. Sure, the pay might be better. Maybe you fly business instead of economy. But job security does not exist, and the free market is far fickler than the federal government. Soon, Scimitar's financial insecurity was going to collide head-on with his sense of grievance.

**ANDY**

On a warm morning in May, I strode into CIA's Langley, Virginia, headquarters for the first time. Hairs tingled on the back of my neck as I crossed the stone seal set into the floor. Ahead of me, beyond the security gates, four pillars framed a garden where southern magnolias dipped their blooms. As I passed by, I nodded toward a galaxy engraved on the marble wall: one star for each officer killed in service since 1947. There is a leatherbound, calligraphy-inscribed book of honor to accompany the memorial, but many of the stars have no names attached. Their identities remain a secret even in death. On that May morning, there were fewer than ninety stars on that wall. Today, following heavy losses during the War on Terror, the figure is around 140.

Amid such solemn splendor, it's impossible not to feel pride — particularly when you're certain your whole life has been building to this moment. Not that it was a smooth ride for me growing up. I was the forgotten stepson from a family broken by murder. When I was a toddler, my father was sarcastic to the wrong man and took a bullet for it. My mother's new husband moved us across the country, from Arizona to rural Pennsylvania. Three-quarters Mexican American and one-quarter Navajo, I was the only brown kid in class. At home, I was the only one in the house who didn't share the same last name.

I spent my childhood, adolescence, and early adulthood in a quest to win affection from my stepdad. It was hard to come by. In Vietnam, my stepdad had been one of the "tunnel rats"—guys whose job involved digging into Viet Cong bases bristling with booby traps. The man had seen it all, and there was no impressing him. But I persevered. I did my chores, of which there were many. On one occasion, I got a C in math and got grounded for an entire summer. The lesson I learned growing up was that to get ahead you had to follow the rules and obey authority, no matter how much you might hate doing so. With this mindset, I forced myself through prep school and into the United States Air Force Academy in Colorado Springs.

At the Academy, it was more rules. We were constantly told that we were the best of the best, that even the worst student there was better than the best student at any state school and blah blah blah. In the run-up to graduation, I told my guidance counselor I wanted to go into intelligence. I loved travel and learning languages; in my junior year, I had even visited Falcon on a language exchange. But apparently, intelligence was not considered a fitting career for an Academy graduate.

"We have ROTC people to do that work," the counselor said, referring to officers graduating from civilian colleges. "At the Air Force Academy, we make pilots."

Once again, the rules were telling me what I had to do, and following the rules was important. Fine, I told myself. If I was going to be a pilot, I wanted to be Top Gun. I even picked out a call sign: Phoenix. (This was before I figured out that you don't pick your own call sign: your buddies wait for you to screw up in some dumb way and then give you the call sign to make fun of you. Like the F-15 pilot out of Tyndall

Air Force Base in Florida who hit a pregnant doe while taking off and will forever be known as Bambi.)

Pilot training was terrible. The days were long and the trainers belittled us constantly, while the exercises themselves taxed my body and my mind. Until you try flying a fast jet, you can't imagine how overwhelming an experience it is. You take caffeine to combat the exhaustion and it makes the motion sickness worse. Despite all this, I did well in the training, but the minimum commitment for a pilot is ten years, and I didn't think I could stomach a decade of that, literally or figuratively. So I quit the pilot track, enduring the inevitable tongue-lashing about duty and service and the good of the nation, and transferred onto the other "prestige" career track in the Air Force: nuclear missileer.

The missile training could not have been more different. It was six months in stunning California wine country, studying up on the destructive power of nuclear weapons—which, to twenty-three-year-old me, sounded rad as hell. I finished in the top three in my class.

Where did that achievement get me? A literal hole in the ground: a bunker at Malmstrom Air Force Base, in the Montana Badlands, where I supervised Minuteman nuclear missiles in their subterranean tubes. My ability to follow the rules made me a natural at the job. Every twelve-hour shift brought a giant checklist: key A goes in lockbox A, code B goes in lockbox B, and so on. The challenge was doing everything exactly right, day after day, without getting lazy or cutting any corners. Which I guess is important when even the tiniest error could lead to Armageddon.

My stellar abilities at box-ticking got me noticed. When the lieutenant colonel in charge of my command post moved on to higher things, he recommended me as his acting replacement. The command had never gone to anyone below a major, and as a lowly first lieutenant, I was two ranks beneath that. But the lieutenant colonel was impressed by my attention to detail. He said he could always count on me to do things right, even when his back was turned. So at age twenty-six, I became the youngest-ever commander of that command post, earned myself a special commendation from the Air Force brass, and wound up in charge of two hundred of the deadliest weapons in history. Plus, the command post was aboveground, so my body could start making vitamin D again. I was soon promoted to captain—still one rank below the usual minimum for the assignment, but ahead of the norm.

On paper, my Air Force career was going great. In practice, I was lonely and miserable. At the command post, I was one of only three officers, and military rules prohibited making friends with any of the enlisted folks. Plus, I had to do all the work of a lieutenant colonel without the rank or the paycheck to match. This was where all my efforts to play by the rules and impress my stepdad had gotten me, and I was sicker than ever of monotony, of discipline, of rules. I decided to move on at my earliest opportunity. When the Air Force announced yet another round of post–Cold War "force shaping" (a military euphemism for layoffs), I jumped at the chance to get out.

Despite it all, I still wanted to serve my country, so I was looking for a way to stay in government as a civilian. In particular, I had my eye on a stint in the Peace Corps. After Montana, travel sounded good. So did helping needy people. So did sweaty sex in tents with hairy hippie women, which I reckoned would be among the perks of a Peace Corps career.

I was filling out my online application in the dingy computer lab at Malmstrom Air Force Base when a big red pop-up appeared.

**YOU MAY QUALIFY FOR OTHER GOVERNMENT POSITIONS.**

**A RECRUITER WILL CONTACT YOU WITHIN 72 HOURS.**

I glanced around at the six other guys checking their email and the one dude in the corner trying to pretend like he wasn't watching porn. Was this some kind of hacker prank? I shook my head and closed the pop-up. *Yeah right,* I thought.

A day later, I got the call. The recruiter didn't say where she was calling from. But she did seem interested in my appetite for international travel and my tolerance for risk. Whoever it was, they FedExed me a plane ticket, a rental car reservation, and directions to a secret facility in Virginia where they told me I was to be interviewed in person.

The building was pretty much like any other suburban office. Inside, it looked like a doctor's waiting room, with maybe a dozen chairs pushed up against the walls. Six pairs of eyes followed me across the room. I sat down. Everyone else there, without exception, was dressed in a black suit. Meanwhile, I had shown up unshaven, my lumberjack shirt untucked over my jeans.

*Well,* I thought, *this is who I want to be now. Take it or leave it.* Nobody returned my smile.

After a few minutes, a heavyset woman of about fifty came out and called my name. We headed further inside for the interview.

"I'm ready to serve," I told her. "But I'm done with rules." Just in case that wasn't obvious.

The interviewer's face was a blank. "Captain," she said, "let's assume you are going to be flying to the DC area regularly. You will need to come up with a plausible reason why. Do you think you can do that?"

I said that I did. I would pretend that I was trying to get a transfer to work for the Air Force as a civilian, which is a common enough transition for former officers.

That was the first lie of my intelligence career.

"Good," she said. "What I am about to say is classified. Do not share it with anyone. Do you understand?"

I said of course I did. She had my military record; she must have known that my assignment at Malmstrom required the highest level of clearance.

"Good. Captain, I'm recommending you as a candidate for CIA's National Clandestine Service."

Finally, somebody got me—and holy crap, it was the goddamn *CIA*! I went from feeling like shit to feeling like a million bucks. This was a new act in my life, and I was determined to play the role perfectly. So as I moseyed into Langley that first day in May, I was gung-ho to save the world or become a star on the wall trying. Either way, I figured, glory awaited.

## JIHI

When you think "CIA officer," I might not be the first person who comes to mind. First off, I was born in a country that has been a US adversary for decades. My dad is a native of that country, although he later naturalized as a US citizen. My mom is American, but rootless from having grown up on military bases all over the world as an Army brat. In addition to being citizens of the world, both of my parents are artists and converts to Soka Gakkai, a Japanese school of Buddhism that emphasizes peace, happiness, and the dignity of individual human beings. When I was a baby, we moved to Hachioji, a suburb of Tokyo, so my parents could learn more about the faith via the nearby Soka University. We lived there until I was six years old.

My name, Jihi, combines two Japanese characters that together mean "to remove suffering and replace with happiness, mercy, and compassion." I tried to live up to the name, at least at first. While going through college and grad school in my home state of Florida, I decided I wanted to do social work with an international element. I worked for a charity supporting refugees who had survived torture, rape, and other trauma. I was the very model of a bleeding-heart hippie. But working with survivors from places like Bosnia and Rwanda gave me a sense of how dangerous a place the world could be, and how easily conflict could erupt. You might think you can trust your neighbors, only to have them show up on your doorstep with a machete. I decided that any alternative to war would be worth pursuing.

Like post–Air Force Andy, I wanted to work in government, to travel, and to help those in need. I applied to every department and agency with a program that might let me do those things, from Health and Human Services to the US Post Office. They all rejected me, and I think I know why. I had a lot of schooling: by age twenty-six, I had picked up a BA (in African American and women's studies), a JD, and a master of social work. But my work history was thin, and federal agencies were looking for real-world experience in their field. The exception, ironically, was the Air Force: they turned me away because they were going through another round of "force-shaping"—the very same redundancy program that gave Andy the off-ramp that eventually led to CIA. Apparently, the universe was putting us on a collision course, whether we liked it or not.

While doing my research into government service, I had seen CIA recruiters at job fairs. But to be honest, they were pretty low on my list. Spy work seemed dangerous, not to mention ethically problematic for a peaceful Buddhist. But I was getting desperate, and I rationalized that part of the point of intelligence is to avoid armed conflict (which is true). I put in an application.

At first, it seemed I was destined to fail once again, but not because of my lack of experience. Military, intelligence, and law enforcement agencies generally don't care about that, because they know they're going to shape you into whoever they want you to be anyhow. With CIA, my worst enemy was...me. I flunked my first phone interview because I forgot the name of a notorious dictator who opposed the United States—not exactly impressive for someone claiming to know a lot about international affairs.

"If you want to work here," the recruiter deadpanned, "you better study up on current events."

"Got it. Sorry."

After doing the necessary reading, I tried again and got through that round. But my troubles were not over. I had to retake my first lie-detector test after freaking out over the question "Have you ever taken material from a government or corporation without permission?" I couldn't stop thinking about the pens and paper clips I had brought home from work over the years.

Somehow, having retaken the polygraph after assuaging my goody-two-shoes qualms, I made it through the months-long recruitment and vetting process. My first day of orientation, I arrived at 6:30 a.m. for a 7 a.m. start, only to find the vast parking lot already packed (it didn't occur to me that CIA operates twenty-four hours a day). Finally, I found a spot about a hundred miles from the building. I had to hustle to make it on time, and to make matters worse, I picked the wrong door. While Andy strolled on in through the ceremonial front entrance, I wound up in the basement, passing such sights as the sweaty gym, the cramped single-chair barbershop, and the awkwardly suggestive hot dog vending machine.

Parking my car and locating the entrance were the least of my worries. During the vetting process, I began to experience episodes where I would start throwing up uncontrollably, at seemingly random intervals. For the life of me, I couldn't keep food down, and as a result I was losing more and more weight. My doctors ran test after test but couldn't figure out what was up. On the Thursday of my first week of orientation, my stomach troubles got so bad that I had to drive myself to the emergency room. The hospital kept me overnight and ran a further battery of tests to see if I had a stomach ulcer. Again, everything came back normal.

I missed class on Friday, but I made it back in on Monday morning. Despite the warm weather, I wore long sleeves, partly because I was chilly from losing all my body fat and partly because I didn't want anyone to see the IV tracks in my arms and draw the wrong conclusions.

I was sitting in the back of the auditorium — near the door, in case I needed to run to the bathroom for the fourteenth time that morning — when I heard a big, hearty laugh from the front of the room. My eyes followed the laugh to its source: a lean, brown-skinned man in a pink shirt. His hair was shortish and curly and his square jaw was covered with something between a five-o'clock shadow and a beard, as if he couldn't decide whether he ought to have facial hair or not. By his appearance, I thought he was probably Arab American. A Buddhist dating a Muslim, I thought... that could work, right?

The Arab guy kept joking and telling stories. The classmates around him hung on his words. Every time he laughed, I felt a little less sorry for myself. I turned to the fellow recruit sitting next to me. "Who is *that*?" I whispered.

"Oh my God," she said, giggling. "That's Andy. Thinks he's hot shit. He keeps saying he's going to become a case officer and hunt down bin Laden."

She rolled her eyes, but I was thinking I could use that kind of confidence in my life right about now. I told myself I would get Andy's number if it killed me. Which, given how stumped the doctors still were, it just might.

## ANDY

My time at Malmstrom was frustrating in more ways than one: let's just say that—believe it or not—military bases in Montana are not exactly a mecca for attractive women. Well, that two-year drought was about to break. I was now the world's newest superspy, and if there's one thing everyone knows about spooks, it's that they get all the action. This was the pinnacle of my life, and I had wild oats to sow. I started dressing as snazzily as I thought I could get away with, dispensing with the tie and donning dress shirts in pink and yellow and turquoise, the top button undone for that laid-back European look. Hello, ladies.

The Monday of week two, I walked into class and saw the cutest girl. Slim, with eyes you could get lost in. But she was dressed like a granny in her long-sleeved sweater, rumpled slacks, and loafers. My brain told me that the only way a woman that beautiful dresses that bland is if she's already been worn down by government work. Plus, she was sitting next to the door, which was where the supervisors usually sat so they could come and go without disturbing the class. Ergo, she wasn't a student: she was an instructor. Ergo, she was off limits. It was a shame, though, because she really was very pretty.

A few weeks later, I was sitting in the front row of the auditorium, between two ladies, trying to persuade one or the other of them—or, if I was really lucky, both—to come dancing with me the following evening. They were having none of it. Most CIA women, I was coming to realize, were more into reading cable traffic and boning up on current events.

"I like to dance."

The voice came from behind me. I twisted around to see the same woman I had noticed on the second Monday. So she wasn't an instructor. Interesting. Either that, or teacher had the hots for *me*. Even more interesting.

"I hear there's good salsa dancing in DC," she said.

"Yeah?" I said, trying to figure out if this really was a teacher hitting on me. "How about tomorrow night?"

"Let's do it. I'm Jihi, by the way."

"Andy."

"Yeah, I know."

The next night, after returning to my cramped apartment outside of DC and donning my best salsa-dancing outfit, I called Jihi, car keys in hand, to tell her I was on my way and ask for directions to her place.

"Uh…" She hesitated. "You know what? I don't think tonight is going to work after all."

I was stunned. What had I done wrong? I knew I had a history of rubbing people the wrong way, but I had only just met this woman. Surely I couldn't have messed it up already?

"Oh, that's a shame," I said. "Could you maybe do tomorrow night?"

"I don't think so."

"Some other night, maybe? Or we could just have a coffee."

"I…I can't. I have to…I have to go." She hung up, leaving me to figure out as best I could what the hell just happened.

## JIHI

I hung up on Andy because, yet again, I had to go puke. All day, I'd been nervous about the date. And when Andy called, asking for directions to a house I had just moved into and barely knew how to find myself, I panicked. That was when I threw up.

As I knelt, retching into the toilet, suddenly everything became clear. It wasn't a stomach ulcer. It wasn't IBS. In fact, it wasn't anything physical at all. The doctors ran some more tests and confirmed it: I was suffering from acute anxiety disorder.

On the one hand, it was a load off my mind to know what was wrong with me. On the other hand, I assumed my career with CIA was over before it had begun. Surely nobody with a psychiatric condition could serve in intelligence. It was a fatal character flaw. When you get damaged goods, you return them as soon as possible.

To my surprise, my supervisors were cool with it. They set me up with a psychiatrist, specially cleared to deal with intelligence officers. They allowed me to defer my basic training while I recovered, and gave me a low-key assignment in the meantime. Knowing what I know now, all of this makes sense. It pays for CIA to take care of its people: the Agency invests a lot in them, even before they begin formal training. Besides, intelligence folks are used to dealing with real human beings, warts and all. They know all too well that nobody's perfect.

Dealing with Andy was a different story. I was so embarrassed by what had happened that I deliberately avoided him. When I saw him in the hallway, I would literally run in the opposite direction. That comedy of errors lasted for a few weeks, until we found ourselves elbow-to-elbow in a cramped all-hands meeting. Summoning all my courage, I apologized to Andy and told him I had been too embarrassed to speak to him.

"So you were avoiding me?" He laughed. "I was avoiding *you*. I thought I'd offended you somehow."

"No, no, no." I was mortified.

"It's okay. But you still owe me an explanation."

I told Andy all about my stomach problems and the anxiety diagnosis.

"I see. In that case, I guess dancing is out. How about we start with, let's say, a cup of tea?"

So we started over, lower-key this time. Our first few dates took place around the CIA campus. We took walks in the gardens. We explored the on-site intelligence museums. We ate together in the CIA food court (actually, to begin with, I watched Andy eat — it took me a while to get confident enough that I wasn't going to throw up all over him).

Unlike other workplaces — and especially government agencies — CIA actively encourages dating within the organization. That way, they figure, both parties know what they can and can't talk about, and there's less chance of a leak. Dating inside comes with big advantages for the parties concerned, too.

The second-worst thing you can do as a CIA officer is fall in love with a foreigner. You can't tell them anything. Even if you are married, you have to embody your cover identity around them for as long as you both shall live. That kind of domestic skullduggery must get old pretty quickly.

So why is that only the second-worst thing you can do? Because in that situation, at least you are required to be consistent in your lies. No, the *worst* thing you can do is fall in love with an American who doesn't work at CIA. Because then there comes a moment of decision. Before marriage, it's the same deal as with foreign spouses: your lips are sealed, or else. Once you are married, you are allowed to make them "witting," meaning that you suddenly reveal the truth about your unusual employment.

"Guess what, honey?" you might say over mai tais at your honeymoon destination of choice. "I'm a spy. I've been lying to you this whole time. Isn't that funny?"

From there, the conversation doesn't tend to go well. We have a friend who spent his whole life preparing to be in CIA. He stayed out of trouble, avoided drugs, studied languages and cultures, got the right degrees, made all the right moves. He made it, and he was so proud. But during the last six months of training, he met the woman of his dreams, whose work had nothing to do with intelligence. On their honeymoon, he made the dramatic reveal.

"Babe, guess what? I'm CIA. Oh, and by the way, we're moving to the Middle East." The marriage lasted all of two years.

Whether American or otherwise, dating anyone outside CIA can get complicated. Dinner, a movie, and an early night is one thing. But if there's a back-to-my-place for something more intimate...there is paperwork. And a lot of it. Because your body and bedroom belong to the US federal government.

So if you know what's good for you, you'll only date inside CIA. Still, it comes with its own challenges. If you are lucky, you might start off by being assigned together. But once one spouse is in a management role, the paranoia about nepotism kicks in and they separate you. So when the next overseas posting comes around, you face another choice: tolerate the long-distance thing, at a cost to your relationship and especially to your children if you have them; or have one spouse "trail" the other, putting their career on pause or abandoning it altogether. Typically, nobody winds up happy. Among such "tandem" couples, divorce is common.

The nepotism worries don't apply to the same extent if you are on different career tracks, which Andy and I very much were. So as we grew closer, we began to dream about one day being posted somewhere together. After all, we were developing complementary skill sets. Someday, maybe, we might make a great team.

# PART II
# FOUNDING FAILURES

## ANDY

"Tell me, Mister Ortega," said the chief inspector, calling me by my alias. "How exactly do you know Major Bondoy? Please be as specific as you can."

The interrogation room was a plain beige box, windowless, with a wiped-clean floor. In the United States, it might have made a decent community-college classroom. But this was not the United States. The chief inspector sat across from me in a leather swivel chair, his bare forearms melting into the Formica. My own chair was made of hard plastic that was digging into my ass. The sooner I could get out of there and get on with my mission, the better.

I tried to look the chief inspector in the eye, knowing that this was the way the men of this country showed their sincerity. "To be honest," I said, "I don't really know the Major at all. We've only met one time."

"I see." The chief inspector scribbled in his notebook, holding his pen in one chubby, liver-spotted hand. "You say you have only met once?"

"That's right." From the corner of the room, I heard the deputy click his teeth. He stared at me and shook his head. Above us, fluorescent lights hummed.

"Interesting," said the chief inspector. "That's not what the Major told us."

My heart leapt as I realized they must have taken my contact into custody, too. *It's okay,* I told myself. *De-escalate the situation. Do what you're trained to do.*

Now the chief inspector's eyes met mine. "Major Bondoy said you were friends," he added.

"Oh well," I said, thinking fast. "We did say that we *felt* like old friends. Because we connected on so many levels. He's married, I'm married. I'm a veteran, he's active duty. We were talking like friends."

"He said you've met three or four times. He said you meet regularly at the same restaurant. And there was something else here about . . . Oh yes. Always on Tuesdays." He grinned. "Is any of this ringing a bell, Mister Ortega?"

*Shit.* Too late, I realized my mistake. In my mind's eye, I saw a prison cell. A reeducation camp. A forced confession. A lifetime of—

*Breathe. De-escalate.*

I noticed that the deputy had left his corner and was moving toward the table.

"Gentlemen," I said, including the chief inspector and the rapidly approaching deputy, "I can't explain why the Major would say that. All I know is—"

The deputy smashed his fist down, shaking the table. "You are a spy!"

"Yes." The chief inspector nodded. "I'm afraid we know all about you."

"A . . . spy?" I said, filling my voice with as much shock as I could muster. "No, no. There's been some mix-up. The Major's first language is not English, so maybe he is confused. Maybe if I could just speak to him—"

"You're never speaking to the Major again!" The deputy jabbed me in the ribs with his index finger, his face so close to mine that I could feel his spittle on my cheeks. "You're never speaking to anyone ever again!" He ranted on and on, accusing me of corrupting a war hero, of ruining Major Bondoy's life, of conspiring to destroy their country. "You CIA dog!"

When the deputy's rage finally subsided, the chief inspector sighed. "Why don't you just admit it, Mister Ortega? It will be easier for you."

I had learned about this ploy. The one where they conjure for you a big red button marked ESCAPE. They put that button right under your fingers and dare you to push it. Except that it's not an escape button. It's a self-destruct button. Admitting to espionage is the fastest route to the gulag . . . or the gallows. I thought of the thirteen dozen stars carved into the wall at Langley. Suddenly that future didn't seem as glorious as it had a year before. I had made one mistake already; I wasn't about to make another. So, no: they would get no confession out of me. Better by far to keep them guessing. Preserve that kernel of doubt in their minds, however tiny.

"But I am not a spy. Honestly, I don't know what you're talking about. Please, you must believe me."

The deputy spat on the floor. "Your government will not protect you," he said. "America does not give a shit about its people. You know this."

The chief inspector waved him back toward his corner. "All right. Here's what's going to happen. You are going to spend some time in a special room we reserve for people like you. After that, maybe you will decide to tell the truth, Mister Ortega."

Before I could fully process his words, the chief inspector's face changed. His expression softened. He made a letter *A* with his hands, signifying "admin time." With that, the chief inspector vanished, and I was back to speaking with Gus, the CIA instructor. Instead of a hostile police station, we were in a conference room on the Farm, CIA's secret training facility.

Gus's body untensed. But he didn't smile.

"Andy," Gus said. "I think you understand now what happened. I think you know why we had to have this session. Am I right?"

I looked at my hands and nodded.

Up to that point, my case officer training had been going well. First came the basic skills everyone needs to survive out in the field: driving fast, shooting straight, staying anonymous. I aced it all. Next was Advanced Field Tradecraft—working human sources, detecting surveillance, executing dead drops, and so on. Standards there are tough, and half of all candidates get cut. We call this process "murder boards," because it's the stage when they convene a panel to kill your career. I aced that portion, too. Finally, this exercise with Major Bondoy was meant to be the capstone on my achievement. Almost nobody got cut at that stage. Having waltzed through basic and survived the murder boards, I figured I was a shoo-in for case officer. Pretty soon, I would be out in the real world, tracking down Osama bin Laden.

I was riding high in my personal life, too. After a few months of dating, Jihi and I decided to move in together. We found an apartment in Falls Church, just outside DC, and I signed the paperwork right before departing for the final exercise. Anticipating the long drive out to the training facility and the glittering career that would surely follow, I treated myself to a Harley-Davidson motorcycle. I was high on life.

The final training exercise took place in a real city in the United

States, but for the purposes of the exercise we were pretending to be in a fictional hostile country, New Reho. My task was to turn a New Rehovian military officer, Major Bondoy—played by a grizzled former CIA case officer—into an intelligence source.

Using training materials provided to me, I researched Bondoy's background. The Major was a talented officer, but at almost fifty years old he had seen practically all his classmates from the military academy promoted above him in the chain of command. The problem was a lingering personal scandal he just couldn't live down. Bondoy had married beneath his class—already a faux pas in New Rehovian culture— and it was an open secret that he had done so because he got the girl pregnant. In New Reho, these strikes against his name were enough to stall his career. He would be stuck as a major until he retired, never earning more money, never rising in prestige. That was a vulnerability. I could use it.

In accordance with standard procedure for intelligence, I created a character of sorts. I was Ruben Ortega, a consultant for American logging companies looking to invest in New Reho. My clients wanted a local fixer to make contacts and grease palms. Under this guise, I approached Major Bondoy. I praised his expertise and strongly implied that the New Rehovian military didn't appreciate his talents. My clients would benefit from his advice, I told him, and they would be eternally grateful. In return, Major Bondoy would be rewarded far beyond what the New Reho military could pay him. He would help his country get richer. He would build a nest egg for his children. The pitch sounded so smooth coming out of my mouth, so convincing.

Bondoy couldn't help but smile. "You are right," he said. "This is exactly what I need. What my family needs."

"Excellent," I said. "My clients will be pleased."

"Okay," said the Major. "Here's what I want to do. Tuesday is my day off. Nobody will miss me. So let's meet always on Tuesdays."

"Fine."

"And let's meet at a restaurant I know on the south side of town, by the river. It's familiar to me. I know the staff."

"Sounds good."

Major Bondoy seemed genuinely excited by this plan. And not just in character, either: behind the mask, I thought I saw a glimpse of the hard-as-nails former case officer, smiling with appreciation for my skill. Maybe I reminded him of a younger version of himself. After years of trying and failing to impress my stepdad, the clouds were parting and the sun was shining through. A little voice inside my head told me I was crushing this exercise.

"Is that okay?" asked the Major.

"Of course," I told him, agreeing to meeting on Tuesdays at his favorite bistro. "Whatever makes you feel most comfortable. Let's maximize your security." I was building rapport, just like they taught me, and it was working. I was so close to recruiting my target, I could almost taste it. I would have done anything to close that deal and get started on my career out in the real world.

So Major Bondoy and I started meeting on Tuesdays at his favorite restaurant. I picked the perfect table: line of sight to the front door, a few steps from the side door, back to a wall so nobody could grab me from behind. Over the course of three or four meetings, I continued to play the relationship perfectly, flattering Major Bondoy until he was putty in my hands. The days were crisp and sunny and I remember Bondoy in his windowpane shirt, smiling at me over the gingham tablecloth. In addition to being impressed, he seemed genuinely to like me. I began to think I might be exceptional at this type of work. I could be one of the best.

But by then it was already over. When I agreed to his chosen restaurant on his chosen day, I surrendered control over venue and timing. That was a cardinal error. The Major and I became predictable. Predictable is suspicious, and in a surveillance society, suspicious is fatal. In the fiction of the exercise, a server at the restaurant earned a little kickback by reporting our meetings to the local police, who in turn were able to bug our favorite table and listen in. That was why the instructors decided that I had gotten myself arrested. When I returned to the Farm, they pulled me in for interrogation.

"Okay," said Gus after bringing the interrogation roleplay to a close. "So, why don't you go talk to your supervisor. He'll tell you where we go from here."

Nick, my supervisor, told me I was in jail and so was Major Bondoy. But I still had to complete the exercise, so they wound the clock back to before my arrest and let me play out the scenario to the end. I was much more careful this time. But the damage was done.

The night before graduation, Nick threw a party at his house to celebrate the end of our training. I was too nervous for drink and chitchat, and I never liked Nick that much anyway, so I spent most of the evening playing with Nick's two dogs.

On the last day of training, I sat in our classroom—the same one where Gus had interrogated me four weeks before—with around a dozen of my classmates. While we waited to be called before the panel that would decide our fate, we systematically shredded all the documents we had used during our exercises (the fine details of CIA training are, naturally, heavily classified). One by one, my fellow trainees were called away, and one by one each of them returned with smiles and high fives.

I was not called. By the end of the day, it was just me sitting alone in a bare classroom. I tried to convince myself that the delay didn't mean I had been cut. But a deeper part of me knew the news must be bad. I was beginning to feel super itchy, which at the time I thought was a weird reaction to stress. Finally, my mentor in the program came in alone. Instead of calling me away, he sat down on the table next to me. He was a great guy, a career officer in the Intelligence Community—who had been drafted in to teach CIA case officers. I wish I could say more about him, but I don't want to jeopardize his work, which remains highly classified.

"So, Andy," he said. "We've kept you waiting awhile. How are you feeling?"

"Honestly, I think I got cut. I think I didn't make it."

He looked me in the eye. "Yeah, that's what the panel decided."

At that moment, the bottom fell out of my world. It was my third strike. My stepdad had ignored me. The Air Force had filed me away underground. And now, CIA was rejecting me. Rage and shame burned like napalm in my chest.

There was a bus leaving the next day to take us all back to headquarters. But screw that. I wasn't going to spend hours cooped up with my successful classmates, listening to them gloat. I stormed back to the motel-style room I was sleeping in and stuffed a wallet and a shirt into my backpack. The rest of my stuff—clothes, shoes, alarm clock, beard trimmer, whatever—I left in a pile in the room. *Let* them *clean it up,* I thought. I imagined Nick personally having to throw out my sweaty boxer briefs and socks. (Later I felt bad when I realized that the task more likely fell on some poor minimum-wage cleaner who had nothing to do with it.)

As I stormed out of the building, I was still feeling itchy. Maybe it was rage? In any case, I got on my Harley and peeled off into the night, heading for anywhere but there.

I found out later that it was my supervisor, Nick, who had swayed the panel against me. He told them I was too erratic, that he wouldn't want to work with me. At the time, it felt like a huge betrayal, and I was furious about it for years afterward. Looking back now, I can understand why he said what he said. Because when it comes down to it, it's better to have a case officer who is consistently mediocre than one who hits a home run one day and gets struck out the next. Because in the espionage game, a single bad play gets you thrown in jail, or worse.

That itchy feeling I had was the final slap in the face. It turned out that Nick's dogs, the ones I spent so much time playing with at the party, had fleas. On my ride home, I could feel their bites burning under my armpits, in my crotch, everywhere. I had finally disobeyed the rules, and this was my reward: a biblical plague.

## JIHI

Anticipating Andy's return the next day, I decorated our new apartment with a celebration banner and balloons. I waited and waited. Finally, late in the evening, my phone rang.

"I got cut," Andy said. His voice was flat.

"Shut up, no you didn't."

A long pause. "I'm coming home."

"Oh shit." I looked around at the decorated apartment. "Tonight?"

"Tonight." He hung up.

There was not a moment to lose. I ripped down the banner and stabbed the air out of the balloons and threw everything in the trash. In the middle of the night, I heard Andy's motorcycle screech to a halt outside. He came in, took a long shower, and collapsed into bed without saying a word.

My training was different from Andy's. To begin with, everyone goes through the same basic instruction in tradecraft. I did surprisingly well there, even if my methods were sometimes unorthodox. One day, I was roleplaying with a contact who casually mentioned that he enjoyed

Campari. For our next meeting, I smuggled a bottle of the stuff into Langley. I didn't know it at the time, but that was very much verboten. Think about it: to a security officer, a glass bottle of alcohol is an explosive encased in shrapnel. The examiner "confiscated" the bottle—but gave me high marks for inventiveness.

This highlights an important distinction when it comes to CIA. When faced with ambiguity, most government officials are trained to fall back on rigid adherence to the rules. If the rules don't resolve the matter, the officials will do nothing until they get orders from someone higher up the food chain.

Intelligence work is different. In the movies, CIA officers have earpieces or eyeglass cameras or tiny trackers with a direct link back to HQ. In the real world, that's baloney. Carrying that kind of gear around would make you massively suspicious. More to the point, spending like that would bankrupt the Agency in a week. When you are out in the field, you're on your own. So a CIA officer must be able to adapt on the fly to anything.

I did so well in basic tradecraft that one of my supervisors suggested I should go to the Farm and try out for case officer. "No thanks," I said. Talking to people all day is not an anxious introvert's idea of fun. Besides, I'm a terrible liar.

Instead, I chose a different career track, that of targeter. At the time, this was a new profession, originally developed for waging the War on Terror. Targeters churn through data—using information and methods that are all deemed by CIA as too classified to talk about—to track down persons of interest to the United States. My training revolved around counterterrorism. But by the time we joined the Agency, it was waking up to the fact that targeting techniques could be used to zero in on more traditional intelligence sources— hostile foreign officials, say.

A targeter's goal in the intel community is twofold. First, you must understand the subject well enough to be able to predict what they will do next. Second, you are looking for any vulnerabilities that you might exploit to get under their skin. Is the target maybe nursing a grievance? Has the nature of their work destroyed their moral compass? Are they addicted to something in short supply—drugs, luxury, prestige? Do they need money? Most significantly of all, do they need help in supporting a loved one, for example with medical bills or college tuition? This brings up an interesting fact about human nature: people generally won't do anything dangerous or illegal just for themselves (outside of a handful of psychopaths you don't want to work with anyway), but they'll move heaven and earth to help a spouse, a parent, or especially a child.

With those two points in place, a field operative can go approach the target in a way that fits in with their pattern of life. When a CIA officer first meets a potential source, they call it a "bump." It's called that because you want it to look as natural as possible, as if you are just bumping into somebody. From there, you can steer the conversation toward the other person's vulnerability.

As you learn more about how intelligence targeting works, you can't help but think about your own pattern of life. During my training, I would leave home at the same time every day, drive the same car, attend weekly briefings at the same time in the same room, leave at the same time, go to the same gym, get Chinese food from the same takeout. It would be so easy to bump me: just sidle up to me in line at the Ming Dragon and get me talking about the kung pao beef.

Inevitably, you begin to feel like an amateur. And it only gets worse, because at the same time, you realize that you can't change your pattern. Not really. Not without disrupting your whole life. What are you going to do? Purposefully have no schedule? Buy five different gym memberships? Six different cars? Shop at ten different grocery stores? It would be untenable.

In fact, what really stands out are those super-rare occasions when you see somebody actually taking these all-but-impossible steps to obfuscate their pattern of life. At that point, you know either they're certifiably nuts or they're working on something very secret indeed.

As my training went on, I got my bearings by walking around CIA's sprawling HQ. The building is organized by region, and most sections are friendly, welcoming, and themed according to geography. It's not unusual to hear salsa music playing from the Latin America section, for example. (Another perk: they have a margarita machine. *¡Órale!*)

On the fifth and sixth floors, however, the music fades. The artwork vanishes. The vaulted stairwell doors, marked only with numbers, are shut and sealed tight with elaborate electronic locks. In fact, there are no handles on the outside: someone inside, watching on CCTV, must deem you worthy of entry. To look at it, you might think this was unused space. Yet here, behind escalating layers of security, is where the Agency's most sensitive work is done. These floors are home to CIA's most elite divisions, the ones that pursue "hard targets"—nations hostile to the United States that go to extraordinary lengths to conceal their secrets from us. As if to underline their difference from the mere mortals who populate the rest of the Agency, these groups are referred to internally not as divisions but as houses.

One of these select departments is Falcon House. The officers here are the best of the best. They hold advanced degrees. They speak tongue-twisting languages. They immerse themselves in their target's culture, even learning to cook local delicacies at home. Up here, there are no frozen-drink machines.

Most of all, these officers possess superhuman amounts of patience. In some other parts of the world, the entire life cycle of an intelligence asset (meaning a human source who gives you information) might be just months: in less than a year, in other words, they've given you everything you need.

Things are different in the hostile territories where the officers on these floors operate. People are watched constantly and trained from birth to be suspicious of Americans. It can easily take years of pains-taking trust-building for a Falcon source to even *start* producing intelligence—that is, if they don't clam up first. For the officers working that source, it's the equivalent of going several years without making a single sale, closing a single deal, or raising revenue by a sin-gle cent. Get it wrong and your career is toast. To work in Falcon House you need nerves of steel and a reputation for infallibility. This was not the place for an anxious Buddhist or a case-officer dropout.

# PART III:

# PLAYING DIRTY

## ANDY

Farm training is intense: so much so that after you're done, CIA offers you three months' leave to recuperate. Most people don't take the whole three months right away, but I did. And I almost didn't go back at all. Having come into the Agency so cocky, the whiplash of my failure with Major Bondoy nearly broke me emotionally. For the whole of my first year, I had focused on making friends only with fellow future case officers. I had chugged the Kool-Aid that said case officers were the crème de la crème, the "tip of the spear," in internal parlance (which, of course, leaves everyone else with the shaft). All the conversations we had were about how awesome we were going to be. After the Farm, I felt too ashamed to continue any of those relationships. I might have been even more lonely than I had been at Malmstrom, if it hadn't been for Jihi. It was Jihi who helped me heal, both physically and emotionally.

"Screw them," I said while Jihi medicated every one of my seventy-plus fleabites with antiseptic and calamine lotion. "I'm not going back. Not ever."

"That's okay, babe," said Jihi. "Do whatever makes you happy."

I looked into her eyes and knew she meant it. I was thunderstruck. In my entire life up to that point, nobody had ever told me I could do "whatever made me happy." No: I had to do what the rules required of me and what authority figures expected of me. Hearing that Jihi would support me no matter what—that was like a fog lifting.

I took my time deciding. I looked around for what else I might do. I still wanted to serve. The Peace Corps was closed off to me now because I had worked in intelligence (the Peace Corps policy on this is unflinching, because it can't afford to be seen as cover for spies). But I could still do AmeriCorps, the domestic equivalent. Maybe I could do that with a view to eventually becoming a teacher. Meanwhile, I did a lot of cooking. I set up the grill on the balcony and became a master of gourmet hamburgers, shrimp skewers, and lobster tails. Life was good, I decided.

Jihi's support during those three months convinced me of two things: One, I wanted to marry her. Two, I needed to stay at the Agency. I knew how difficult it was being a couple in which one half was in and the other out. Jihi's career was going well and she was working hard. If I wanted to be close to her on a regular basis, I needed to be inside CIA.

So I stayed: this time, not out of some grudging sense of duty, but because I chose to. Psychologically, this was huge, even though the quality of our diet took a nosedive now that I didn't have time to grill surf 'n' turf every night. (Sidebar: I know one other guy who was cut from the program at the same time as me, a fluent Farsi speaker named Arash. When he heard the news, he grabbed a cigar and a glass of scotch and disappeared into the woods. The police found him hours later just staring into space. He never returned to the Agency. Last I heard of him, he was working as an international cocktail mixologist, dividing his time between Miami and Paris. I stand by my choice...I guess.)

I was back, but nothing could change the fact that the elite ranks were forever closed to me. Instead, I worked as a staff operations officer—a SOO, pronounced like the girl's first name—essentially a program manager. Mostly, I was a desk jockey, providing administrative support to case officers and higher-ups. I would move money around, file reports. If somebody needed to pitch for funding for an operation, I would be the one to put together the PowerPoint deck. Occasionally I would get to travel, but it was almost always as nothing more than a glorified courier, bringing people things too classified for CIA to let us talk about. It wasn't quite as predictable as Malmstrom, but it was almost as deadening to me emotionally.

As a SOO, I would never be assigned to deal with big strategic threats like Falcon. Instead, I was relegated to second- and third-tier work in countries of lesser strategic importance to the United States. In these garden spots, I worked against drug dealers and human traffickers and weapons smugglers and jayvee terrorists—all of whom, I came to realize, existed in symbiosis in the same rotten ecosystem.

At CIA, being a SOO is far from prestige work. The dream for any intelligence officer is to generate information that gets shown to the president of the United States, and nobody is going to waste the president's time with details about the financier of a human-trafficking ring in Africa. These guys are bad news, sure, but they're not a strategic threat to the US the way, say, Falcon is.

Now that I cared way less about my work, I took every opportunity to goof off and hang out with my girlfriend. During an average workday, Jihi and I probably spent an hour or two together, between breakfast, lunch, coffee, and just walking the hallways. In the meantime, I would send her cute messages on our internal chat system.

Where I stood out was in the advice I would give to case officers. Usually, SOOs in my position would just administrate, leaving the actual conduct of the cases up to the folks in the field. But I figured I could be of more use. I had passed the Farm, after all, even if I wasn't certified. So I would offer operational guidance to the case officers I worked with. I developed a reputation for out-of-the-box suggestions. Most of these were rejected out of hand, but occasionally one would be accepted and would work.

On one occasion, I was supporting a case officer I'll call Sundeep, who was working against a hard target with ambitions in the nuclear realm. Unlike the vast majority of case officers at the time, Sundeep was not white, and because of this he experienced less suspicion and enjoyed more access in this nation than did most case officers. He had used this advantage to develop a budding friendship with an important official who was working on the nuclear program. Unfortunately, the official seemed less interested in talking about his work and more interested in allowing the American to buy him expensive dinners.

How to move the official to the next stage? Sundeep thought a well-timed "gift" would do the trick. Should he just bribe the guy straight up? No, I said. That would risk offense. He needed to offer something unique, not overtly connected to the United States. I knew that solid gold carried a lot of value culturally in that part of the world. How about a historic coin? Something the official could show off and brag about. I figured out the logistics of having someone buy the coin untraceably in Europe and ship it to Sundeep's buddy in a way that would be equally untraceable, thus making it safe for him to receive it. The official was delighted: so much so that he aspired to become a collector.

"I can get you more," Sundeep told him. "But you need to give me something in return."

My idea was a hit. The breakthrough meant that the case was moved to a level of confidentiality where, as a mere SOO, I was no longer cleared to work on it. Before, I might have been frustrated at this loss of access; now, I was so checked out that I was just relieved to have it off my plate.

Around the same time, I was supporting a case against an extremist group with links to al-Qaeda. One of our offices in the region had found a possible lead: a shopkeeper they suspected of laundering funds to be used to make propaganda films—the kind where there's a bunch of chanting and dudes in ski masks doing assault courses.

The shopkeeper wasn't a member of the terror group. He spoke only money. He didn't know personnel movements, weapons shipments, propaganda, communications, or anything else. The people who did know that stuff were usually too secretive to track down directly. But I thought maybe we could identify the shopkeeper's contact in the terror group, start tracking him, and penetrate the local cell that way—just like Osama bin Laden's courier was tracked.

Could the shopkeeper lead us to an actual terrorist? The local office was reluctant to risk one of its own case officers on what might be a wild goose chase. So they called me in. I had Farm training but wasn't a case officer; in other words, I could do the job, but I was disposable. And since I look anything but Anglo, we reckoned the shopkeeper would likely be less suspicious of me.

I created a story for the operation: I was a representative of a big multinational crime syndicate, heavily involved in smuggling drugs through the region. The story would be that my associates and I needed to move money for paying off crooked politicians. I flew in and stayed in a hotel whose cramped rooms reeked of tobacco. Outside the window, dead animals rotted in the street while barkers hawked beer, SIM cards, baseball caps, you name it. This was the kind of setting I'd gotten used to since becoming a SOO.

The store looked like a million others in this teeming megacity: part pawn shop, part dollar store, part currency exchange. The place was packed floor-to-ceiling with cigarette cartons, bagged candy, second-hand phone batteries, stuffed animals contorted into clear plastic bags. In the corner was a fridge with cans of coffee and condensed milk, although I wouldn't want to consume anything from it, given how unreliable the electricity was there. Everything was covered in a patina of dust and grime. A sign over the register read, MONEY TRANSFER. That was indeed the guy's main business, although he wasn't exactly Western Union.

However urgent a case is, field intelligence officers will usually resist the temptation to dive right in and demand the information they want; that would only raise suspicion, and at best the source would clam up. At worst, well...this is al-Qaeda we are talking about. Instead, the first order of business is to build rapport and trust with the source. In this case, I needed the shopkeeper to believe I was just as much of a lowlife as he was.

"I'm trying to transfer some money," I said. "Can you help with that?"

"Oh yes." He went into what was obviously his standard spiel. "We specialize in transferring money anywhere in the world. You can pick any currency you want. We have really competitive rates. We can—"

I cut him off. "Well, see, I'm less worried about your rates. I'm more concerned with doing this transaction discreetly. You don't need to know about me or what I do. I don't want anyone to know where the money came from or where it went. Or what it's for. Do you know what I mean?"

The shopkeeper didn't hesitate. "Yes, I understand. We can make sure of all that."

"How much?"

Again, there was no hesitation. "Discretion fee is 12 percent."

This was pretty standard. But I feigned shock. "Twelve? Why so much, my friend?"

"We are very secure here. We run everything through many countries. To cleanse it, you understand."

"How do I know this works? Have you done it before?"

"Many times."

And now came my real question.

"Many times?" I asked. "For whom?"

The shopkeeper glanced around. Mosquitoes chased each other through the dusty air. A cockroach darted under the refrigerator. Out on the street, mopeds revved and honked as they made their way through the soup of industrial smog.

"For some... Muslim friends of mine. They sometimes pass through. They like to keep things discreet because they are not welcome here."

That was it: as much of a lead as I was going to get. I nodded. "I see. Good. We will be in touch."

Armed with only vague words — "some Muslim friends of mine... not welcome here" — I had to make the case for an expensive surveillance package: a suite of measures to track and tail him. There was a mountain of paperwork to climb, a bunch of asses to kiss. It took four layers of approval just to get the money allocated; actually spending it would mean still more forms, more meetings.

It occurred to me how different this was from the way our enemies worked. If they wanted to do an operation — a kidnapping, a bombing — they could just do it. Terrorist cells, like al-Qaeda, were close-knit and self-sufficient. They had all the skills they needed right there in the cell: comms, leadership, bomb-making, muscle, transportation. They didn't have to put in a form requesting specialist support from the surveillance department or the tech team. As well as being quicker, this approach meant that nobody outside the cell—not even those above them in the command structure—needed to know the details of their operations. This was the model Osama bin Laden used to conceal his activities after 9/11, and it was a major reason why it took so long for US intelligence to track him down.

Finally, after more than a month of bureaucratic wrangling, I got the go-ahead. Step one was to monitor the shopkeeper. We found his likely contact within the al-Qaeda franchise: a name that had been flagged a few times in different countries in the region. We knew the shopkeeper occasionally spoke with this person. We monitored their methods of communication, but neither of them ever connected with anyone else of interest. We figured that he had different communication methods for different purposes, or else he conducted those meetings face-to-face: either would have been standard operating procedure for a terrorist. So, at still more expense, we had the contact followed around town for a week or two. He went to the laundromat, the grocery store, the internet café, the bar, the brothel, but he never went anywhere or met anyone remotely interesting to us.

Maybe he was the wrong guy. Maybe he was operational only part time. Maybe he knew he was being watched. In a sense, it doesn't matter, because we had no other leads: it was that guy or bust. The trail died with him, and his file went on the shelf with all the other dead ends.

As the US discovered in its decade-long quest to track down bin Laden, this is part of how terrorist cells stay secure: they only allow the enemy to see one person at a time. In any given terrorist cell, typically only one member communicates with the broader organization of which they're a part. Anyone seeking to take down the cell will have to nail that specific person, who is likely to be extremely paranoid. Even if you take down that cell, it's just one of dozens or hundreds. Each will have a single point of contact with the next layer in the organization, but most likely they only communicate on a specific phone number using a specific code name, both of which—the phone number and the code name—will go silent the moment anything untoward happens. If you want to dismantle a terrorist group, you have to do it painstakingly, one link at a time.

If you've seen any *Mission: Impossible* or James Bond movies, it might be tempting to believe we can use technology to get around this problem. Nope.

A few months after I shelved the shopkeeper's file, I was called in to help with another terrorist case. A US ally in the region was asking for assistance in taking down the leaders of a hard-line splinter group that had emerged in our ally's sphere of influence. In our case, the country manager at Langley had reasoned that by helping our friends out, we could earn brownie points with this allied intelligence service. They called me in because I was the master of pitch decks: I could make a presentation that would appeal to all the overlapping interests: local, regional, counterterrorism, counterintelligence.

We got the funding and began corralling all our intelligence resources, from the likes of the military, the National Security Agency, the National Geospatial-Intelligence Agency, and the National Reconnaissance Office. It was like drinking from a firehose. There was one big leader—a former financier turned mastermind—and maybe three senior lieutenants. Did we know their names? Yes. In fact, we knew like twenty names and aliases each was thought to use. Did we know their communication methods? Yes. In fact, we knew dozens of communication methods they'd used at various times. The same went for vehicles they used, buildings where they stayed, and prostitutes they frequented. You start to see the problem: the technology spits out way too much data. To make any sense out of it, you need people on the ground who can interpret it for you.

Meanwhile, we were picking up more and more chatter about the splinter group. Human sources were talking about a "meeting" in a big city with "important men" in attendance. A meeting could mean a *jirga*—a gathering of the elders. It could mean a wedding. Either way, this might be an opportunity to take down a bunch of the leaders all at once.

At that point David, the case officer on the ground, called me. "How do you feel about coming out for a week? You could see what our friends here are doing in real time."

My heart sank. Maybe I should have been flattered. But all I could think of was the long flight in economy class, the crummy hotel they'd put me up in, the time away from Jihi—all to do the same busywork they made me do at Langley.

Jihi had a better attitude. "This is great news!" she said. They had asked for me. Didn't I want to work in the field? Which I guessed I did.

My second day there, we invited the local intelligence service to come show us their file on the splinter group's leadership. Since I wasn't official, protocol dictated that I couldn't let them see my face. David, who was their official liaison, met them in one room and ferried their file to me behind another layer of security. The file was thin. Local reports repeated the chatter about a "meeting" featuring "important men." There were a few phone numbers, some receipts for seemingly random items. That was about it.

Some of this was down to poor training. Some was probably corruption—the local government didn't have a good record there. Still, I could sympathize. Their sources were peripheral people, like the shopkeeper I had worked on. They wouldn't know the details of the meeting. In fact, we were lucky they even knew it was happening. David went out to give the locals specific questions to ask their sources: questions of the who, where, what, why, when, and how variety. But we knew we were unlikely to get much more out of them than the local service had on its own.

Days later, while I was still in the city with David, suicide bombs exploded at two hotels, killing several people. When they said "meeting" and "important men," that had been code for attacks. But lacking almost any insight into the cell, we didn't know that.

It was *Groundhog Day*. Dead end after dead end. Meanwhile, the bombings and kidnappings and propaganda continued. And I wasn't the only one having this experience. Back in Langley, over lunches and coffees in the food court, I would listen to Jihi and her targeter friends vent about how tough terrorist cells were to crack, and all the death and destruction we were powerless to stop. We could get to the courier, the money launderer, the driver, but seldom to the real bad guys. For years, this was my life, and it looked like it might be my whole CIA career: smacking my head against the brick wall of terrorist cell after terrorist cell.

# PART IV
# DUTY CALLS

## SCIMITAR

To Scimitar, it must have seemed as if he'd landed on his feet. His new job with big finance had taken him outside the United States, to a big city closer to Falcon. In a single bound, he had leapt from the windowless beige of Langley to an office with a commanding view over the metropolis he now called home. His salary in this new role eclipsed his Agency pay. And he still enjoyed the thrill of the chase, even if his targets now were white-collar criminals instead of Falcon secret agents.

As well-off as he now was, however, Scimitar could not resist making a little extra by playing both sides. For a small kickback, he would pass information about the bank's investigations to corrupt Falcon officials, enabling them to extort some money from the fraudsters in exchange for turning a blind eye.

More seriously still, Scimitar's employer had amassed evidence that he was working with Falcon intelligence. The purpose of these contacts was not clear—yet. The bank reported its findings to the FBI, but apparently the feds did not pursue Scimitar at this stage. A couple of years into Scimitar's tenure, the bank had amassed enough evidence of his wrongdoing. They fired Scimitar.

It could not have come at a worse time. The cost of living in Scimitar's new hometown was eye-watering. It was the height of the financial crash, and his sons were inching closer to college. How would he pay for all this? What was he supposed to do?

That's the kind of vulnerability that intelligence agencies worldwide pray for, and Falcon intelligence lost no time in exploiting it. They activated one of their assets in Scimitar's new hometown: a corrupt official who had been working for them for years. The ex-bureaucrat approached Scimitar with a business proposal: they would become middlemen, facilitating contact between Falcon officials and the foreign banks who needed their clearance to operate. With Scimitar's experience in the finance industry and the ex-official's contacts in Falcon, they could clean up. The two men set up a company together to pursue this opportunity.

The company was a fake, and Scimitar knew it. Having kept up his contacts with Falcon intelligence this whole time, he was contemplating a much more lucrative venture. The company was a fig leaf for that scheme.

Two weeks later, Scimitar and the ex-bureaucrat were in Falcon together, supposedly schmoozing a couple of representatives from a Falcon financial regulator. As Scimitar likely already knew, in reality they represented a very different organization.

Toward the end of dinner, the two Falcon representatives sent Scimitar's business partner out for a cigarette break. We can reconstruct the conversation that followed.

"Your résumé is interesting to us," said one of the representatives. "Your real one, I mean."

"You see," said the other, "we do the same type of work."

"I understand." Scimitar kept his face expressionless, using the emotion-suppression techniques he had learned in training at CIA.

"We are here to offer you a gift."

"Gifts, plural."

"Money."

Scimitar thought for a moment. He should get up right now, follow his business partner out that door, never speak to these people again. But then what would John and Jacob do for college?

"How much?"

"Seventy-five thousand dollars. US."

"At first."

It wouldn't cover college, not on its own. But it would help lessen the burden. And maybe if he earned their trust, there could be more where that came from.

"We want to look after you," said the first representative, seeming to read Scimitar's thoughts.

"You *and* your family," said the other.

"All we need is some of the knowledge you possess."

Scimitar knew what that meant. During his years at the Agency, he had served as a case officer in Falcon. He had retired a few years ago; but the information in his head remained very relevant to officials in this "type of work."

Sharing that information would be so easy. He still had it all squirreled away in his head. If he was only willing to hand it over, John and Jacob would be set up for college, maybe even debt-free.

Being in need of funds is one thing. But there are many ways to earn a better living. Betraying your country, selling secrets, risking people's lives—physically, it's easy, provided you don't get caught. But psychologically, could Scimitar live with himself?

He must have known what he ought to do in this situation—it's drummed into every Intelligence Community employee. If a foreign intelligence service approaches you, you report it to Security right away. What you absolutely do *not* do is agree to help.

But for $75,000 in cash . . . and maybe more further down the line . . .

We will never know what went through Scimitar's mind that evening in Falcon. What we do know is that he accepted the offer. And with that, Scimitar became a Falcon mole.

## ANDY

While I continued to grapple with terrorism at work, in my personal life I tasked myself with a different mission, one that I hoped would have a much higher probability of success: propose to Jihi, and make sure it's a delightful surprise. Against a targeter as good as Jihi, such an operation required careful planning. It started with a campaign of what CIA refers to as covert influence. To throw Jihi off the scent, I started bad-mouthing the institution of matrimony at every opportunity.

"Only crazy people get married," I'd say, citing the example of my mom, who had finally gotten a divorce from my stepdad a couple of years before. "Me? I'll never get married." It seemed to work, although this phase of the op was not airtight: I discovered later that Jihi had looked at my browser history and found out I was researching engagement rings. Luckily, the friend at the Agency that Jihi confided in about her discovery propped up my disinformation campaign.

Phase two was to recruit an asset. Jihi's dad is unusual in some ways — like her mom, he's an artist and a convert to Buddhism — but in other ways he's a deeply traditional Latin father. So before I proposed to Jihi, I went to him and formally asked his permission. That pleased him, but the icing on the cake was when I told him that I planned to change my last name to Bustamante and pass it on to our kids.

Joel Bustamante had two daughters and no sons, and I knew it bothered him to think of the name dying with him. Meanwhile, my own last name never meant much to me. It wasn't even my birth father's original name: he was adopted as a small child. On top of that, when my mom married my stepdad (the hard-ass Vietnam vet), she took his last name but didn't change mine to match. When my sisters were born, they got my stepdad's last name, too. In our small town, there was a collectible teddy bear store that happened to have the same name as my family's last name. It became a memorable annual family trip for my parents and sisters, but for me it was a solid reminder that I was always the odd man out, and they never let me forget it.

By contrast, Jihi's parents represented the kind of loving, supportive family I never experienced growing up. When I volunteered to carry on the Bustamante name, I made an ally for life. Joel celebrated in the two ways he knew best: art and jokes. He designed a Bustamante coat of arms, featuring thirteen balls, representing the twelve generations he had traced back plus me. It was accompanied with a few paragraphs of Spanish worthy of Cervantes: "Whereas the gentleman Andrew hath proffered his balls unto the family Bustamante, the family Bustamante hereby acceptest said balls unto its bosom. What balls profferest thou? Thine balls are..." You get the picture. He even put the coat of arms on a T-shirt for me.

Only later did I realize what a pain in the ass it is for a man to change his last name. Every bank, insurer, and government agency assumes you are attempting some kind of fraud and makes you jump through all kinds of hoops—which in my case was ironic, since everything else they knew about me was a lie. But I persevered. It was worth doing as a symbol of my commitment to Jihi. Besides, I figured it would be good for me operationally, because two last names would make it twice as hard for anyone trying to track me, the same way multiple identities helped conceal the terrorists I was trying to find.

With Jihi's dad on board and my disinformation campaign in full swing, everything was in place for phase three: the big reveal. I arranged for Jihi's parents to fly up from Florida and my mom to drive down from Pennsylvania, ostensibly to visit Washington's cherry blossom festival. Cherry blossoms carry a deep meaning for Jihi from her time growing up in Japan, and the original DC cherry trees were themselves a gift from the Japanese government. I entrusted the ring to Jihi's mom in case Jihi went through my stuff looking for clues. Once a targeter, always a targeter.

We spent a couple of hours walking around the Tidal Basin, admiring the blooms. Then I got down on one knee, and Jihi...shook her head? Oh my God, how had I misjudged this? Was Jihi the Major Bondoy of my love life?

No. She was shaking her head in disbelief at having fallen for my deception. As to the marriage thing, she was into it.

We got married about a year later. We rented a house on North Captiva Island, off the Gulf Coast of Florida, and held the ceremony on the beach, combining elements of Jihi's Japanese culture and my Navajo heritage. As we headed off on a honeymoon cruise of the Caribbean, we knew our lives would never be the same again. We just didn't know yet in how many ways.

## JIHI

Like Andy, I was destined to wind up frustrated by my assignments. Unlike him, it had nothing to do with the impenetrability of America's adversaries, and everything to do with plain, old-fashioned bureaucracy.

Following training and certification, I was assigned to a country

CIA refers to as a hard target—meaning, essentially, one that is both secretive and hostile toward the United States. Let's call it Badger. As in my training, my primary work product was targeting packages: reports detailing a subject's pattern of life and suggesting ways of getting to them. Sometimes these concentrated on specific individuals. Other times, they focused on organizations within Badger's government. Still other times, they were grab bags of folks the case officers might be interested in pursuing.

Frankly, we had to take what we could get: Badger's paranoia made it too dangerous even to think about targeting its own officials or military officers on their home turf. We had to approach them outside of Badger, which meant I would be working with case officers in a variety of third countries.

This work was just as tough as the counterterrorism cases I had trained on, but for opposite reasons. Counterterrorism is like looking for needles in haystacks: you get tons and tons of information, most of it useless. For example, as Andy was finding out around the same time, a terrorist might have twenty different communication methods, all generating data, of which only a tiny slice is of any interest.

Whereas terrorists are chaotic, hard targets are disciplined—brutally so. With Badger, we are talking about the kind of nation where, if a government official steps an inch out of line, their whole family could suffer. A country like that is a black hole for information. For a targeter, it's like looking not for a needle in a haystack, but for a grain of sand in outer space.

You learn to live on scraps, and turn those scraps into something more nutritious, using patience and creativity. Let's say you get a single name: someone who may or may not be a Badger intelligence officer. After weeks and weeks of searching, maybe you find a critical piece of data from 2007 with a similar-sounding name. So now you know this person (or somebody with a similar name) was in, let's say, Stockholm in 2007. Can you find the hotel where this maybe–intelligence officer stayed? Could there be a record of the credit card they used to pay for room service? Was that credit card ever used anywhere else? You progress in this way, joining dots separated by millions of miles until a constellation comes into view.

Most of my work took place on a computer terminal at Langley, but I did manage to persuade my bosses to send me overseas to debrief a former Badger military commander, now living outside of Badger. CIA had helped him when the Badger government got too close to learning that he was a US asset. Now, he was working a nine-to-five office job for a middling income. Occasionally, American intelligence officers would show up and remind the commander that he used to be someone by grilling him about his previous occupation.

Not surprisingly, depression had kicked in, and the commander had become an alcoholic and a gambling addict. He had a reputation among CIA people for being grumpy and less than forthcoming. I felt sorry for the people assigned to babysit him; they had to try to keep the commander's addictions under control and make sure he didn't show up to our meetings drunk.

On the trip with me was a CIA interpreter, Dianna. She was a naturalized US citizen who spoke multiple languages. Like me, she wasn't one of those people who had always dreamed of working for CIA; she had done a variety of different jobs before her husband, who was an analyst at the Agency, suggested it to her. As a result, I found Dianna more approachable than most linguists I had encountered. She was also more forthcoming with observations and advice beyond the remit of a traditional translation.

Dianna warned me that the commander knew some English, so I would have to watch what I said to avoid giving offense or setting off his neuroses. In particular, family was a sore spot for him. We had managed to help his wife and son, but now they blamed him for their reduction in status. Meanwhile, the rest of his family was still in Badger, and God only knew what their life was like. I would have to ask about certain members of his extended family who were also prominent in Badger. To cushion the blow, Dianna suggested that I avoid mentioning their relationship to him and just refer to them by name and job title—not as Uncle John, but as General Doe.

We also discussed the challenge of my being young and a woman; in Badger's culture, as in many masculine cultures worldwide, these were two strikes against me. Dianna suggested that I go out of my way to demonstrate outward deference to the men in the room, including the commander himself.

Throughout the debriefing, which lasted two days, I made a great show of deferring to my supervisor, who was a man and older. At the conclusion of each topic, I would nod to him, as if seeking permission to go on. (To underline the point, it also helped that he was a huge guy—a former bodybuilder, in fact.) Just as importantly, I told the commander again and again how grateful I was for his assistance. This helped frame me, in his eyes, as a respectful person who knew her place.

During breaks in the questioning, Dianna would clarify certain points for me. She would explain the nuance behind the way the commander expressed himself: what his choice of this word instead of that one said about his emotional state, for example. Like how in English someone might refer to a police officer as either a "cop" or a "pig," with drastically different connotations. This, in turn, helped steer my questions in a productive direction.

It worked. Whereas in previous interviews the commander tended to offer curt, single-word answers, this time he opened up, offering color and context that helped flesh out CIA's understanding of Badger's secretive inner machinations.

During downtime, I took long walks with Dianna up and down the waterfront. We bonded over novels and *Star Trek* fandom and quickly became friends. It turned out that her husband was often posted overseas (his skill set was very focused on one particular small country, so he was there more or less constantly), which meant Dianna was often at a loose end. Back in Washington, we would meet up for movie nights. Better yet, she was a phenomenal baker, responsible for the most delicious and fattening butter cakes I have ever tasted. In friendship terms, I felt I'd hit the jackpot.

But that overseas trip was the exception, not the rule. On a typical day, my only direct interactions were with my fellow targeters, and that posed serious problems. My office mates were brilliant, and they taught me a huge amount, but they were all doing the exact same work as me. Somewhere out there, we knew, case officers were busy working on the same cases we were. They might as well have been in outer space. If you wanted to communicate with a case officer, you had to do it in writing, over a secure messaging system. Sometimes, I would see at 3 p.m. on a Friday that a target would be in range of a particular case officer. I would send the case officer a message, but it was too late. Even if the case officer saw the message, I didn't know what else they had going on. They might be away or busy. And that was when you had a specific piece of intel. If you just wanted to brainstorm — essential to generating the kind of creative ideas we needed when working against a target as hardened as Badger — you were generally out of luck.

Because of this stovepiped way of doing business, we missed opportunities. Working face-to-face with case officers on the same cases might have taken care of the problem. But single-discipline monocultures were just the way it had always been done, and in intelligence at that time, tradition counted for a lot.

Toward the end of my stint working against Badger, my manager made matters worse through sheer inefficiency. She was supposed to review and approve my targeting packages within a few days, but this line manager would sit on them for up to five weeks. She waffled for so long that the target would have come and gone, been promoted or demoted, changed their status or communication methods, or all of the above. I would be left having to redo the whole thing. This time-wasting happened over and over, to the point where I got so sick of it that I would have taken literally any other assignment. With the support of my supervisor (who knew what this line manager was like), I went from office to office, offering my services, until at last I clinched what I saw as a prime overseas posting, in an island nation.

By early summer, I had spent months reading up on the assignment, meeting my future colleagues, and developing my new work persona—typically one of the final tasks you undertake before deploying. Meanwhile, Andy was working on securing his own assignment to the same place. It seemed like we might be close to the dream of getting posted overseas together.

Then, one day, my supervisor—the one I liked, the ex-bodybuilder—appeared in my cube with a puzzled look on his face. He told me there was some issue with my assignment.

"What kind of an issue?"

He shrugged. "That information, it would seem, is above my pay grade. All I know is, you are supposed to report to door NCC-1701."

My mind reeled. Was I in trouble? What had I done wrong? Did this mean that Andy and I would be separated again? Could we still...

Wait a minute.

"Did you say NCC-1701?"

"I did."

"Isn't that Falcon House?"

"You know, I believe it is."

I knew it was. I had been told to report to the same place a couple of years before, when I was sent there for a two-month training rotation during the on-the-job portion. Falcon House's second-in-command wanted to give me the once-over before letting me loose in her hallowed halls. I remembered standing at the huge, blank door, staring up at the security camera while the secretary on the other side decided whether or not to buzz me in. At that time, the second-in-command was a small, slight woman, and her office was completely dark except for a single lamp on the desk that cast dramatic shadows across her face. The biggest mystery of all was how she could work like that without eyestrain.

As if that were not cloak-and-dagger enough, halfway through our meeting another officer walked in and told her that he needed the money for such-and-such a case. The second-in-command opened a drawer in her desk and counted out a Scrooge McDuck amount of money in crisp, hundred-dollar bills, which she handed over in a Ziploc baggie. My jaw hit the floor. At the time, that much money would have funded one of Andy's counterterrorist cases for the best part of a year. But the second-in-command didn't seem fazed. She turned back to me and said something like, "What were we talking about? Oh yes, where do you see yourself going in your career?"

Andy and I tell people all the time that CIA is not like the movies. And most of the time, it's not. But that meeting was straight out of *Casino Royale*. In my mind, it deepened the mystique of Falcon House even further. One of its top brass casually hands over a pile of cash right in front of some junior scrub she didn't know from a hole in the wall. Imagine what she did when I wasn't in the room. Imagine what Andy or I could do with resources like that at our fingertips.

My training rotation in Falcon House turned out to be just like that initial meeting. The whole place was dark, literally, as if they were try-ing to save on electricity. When they weren't looking over your shoul-der to check you were working, people stood in the shadows, whispering to each other. The information you were given was so compartmental-ized that you never knew what was going on or why you were being asked to do any given task. In short, it sucked. When the two months were done with, I couldn't wait to leave.

Now I was back in the same office, behind door NCC-1701. There was a new second-in-command, a big, jovial guy who ushered me in with a smile. The office now looked more normal, with fewer books and more pictures of the guy's family. Plus he had turned the lights on, which must have been better for his eyes.

"I have talked to your supervisor. I know you've been assigned."

"That's right." Where was this going?

"Yes. Well, we would like to assign you somewhere else. We've had unexpected developments."

"What kind of developments?"

His face fell. "A friendly intel service has reported that we may have been compromised."

I frowned. In the business of secrets, you never want to hear the word "compromised." It can mean a lot of things—and all of them are bad. A technical compromise could be a cyber-hack; a human compro-mise could be a double agent; an intel compromise could be false reporting. If it's an operational compromise, that could literally mean the difference between life and death. My anxiety spiked and my stom-ach cinched as quickly as the thought hit my mind.

"We are trying to confirm details. This is the first we've heard about a possible compromise, but we are taking it seriously. In the meantime, we need somebody to go out to the region and start building new operations. We need a new set of reporting sources that are fully separated from our current records in case this compromise proves to be true. What do you think?"

"Where would I be based?" I asked, worried that my shiny new assignment was about to be replaced with a posting in some hellhole. But to my relief, he said the name of a city that we will call Wolf.

Suffice it to say, Wolf is not in Falcon, but it's in the same region and it's known for its vibrant nightlife. Suddenly this was looking like an okay deal. The only catch was that Andy might have to become a trailing spouse, which I wasn't sure he would like.

By the end of the meeting, my head was spinning. When I got back to my cube, I messaged Andy. "You'll never believe what just happened," I wrote. I told him all about the summons and the meeting over at Falcon House.

"You're kidding, right?"

"Nope. Why do you say that?"

"I just had the exact same thing happen to me."

# PART V
# IMPOSSIBLE TASKS

## ANDY

I had an earlier run-in with Falcon intelligence. Not that I knew it at the time. In 2001, in my junior year at the Air Force Academy, I was selected for an exchange program that involved spending nine weeks at a swanky school in the Falcon capital, Kestrel. I was already chafing against the rules, and I spent the whole time dressing down, not shaving, and generally distancing myself from the military. Looking back, knowing what I know now, I can see that was a vulnerability ripe for exploitation.

We had three tutors, all female and all selected not so much for their teaching ability as for their likely appeal to young American cadets rich in testosterone and poor in common sense. I developed a particularly close relationship with the oldest of the three. One day, we were walking together down a main commercial street in Kestrel when she steered our conversation, improbably, onto the subject of the alphabet.

"As a teacher, letters are so interesting to me," she said. "Numbers, too."

"Yes, absolutely," I said, eager for a deep dive into all things Falcon.

"Letters and numbers are important in your work, too, aren't they? Like how you name your planes. F-117, for example. On its own, that means one thing, but if you add an *A* after it, it means something different. Isn't that right? Why do you need that extra letter?"

The F-117A was a variant of the F-117 Nighthawk: she was asking me about a stealth fighter. My teacher was approaching me as a potential source of intelligence, something I would later learn to do myself at CIA. But back then I was utterly clueless. All I remember feeling is embarrassed that this hot older woman seemed to know more about US planes than I did. If I had known the difference between the F-117 and the F-117A, I would have told her. As it was, I sheepishly told her I didn't know. She changed the subject and it never came up again. I guess she reported to her handler that I was every bit as much of an idiot as I looked. At any rate, it wasn't until I got home and was debriefed by an Air Force security officer that I realized that anything suspicious had taken place. From a vulnerability point of view, she got the right guy. It was just their bad luck that I knew nothing.

Now, years later, Jihi and I were being asked to take on Falcon intelligence. It was rare enough to be assigned to the field in our respective roles as a targeter and a SOO, but for both of us to be sent together on the same mission was practically unprecedented. It wasn't yet clear why the Falcon House leadership were doing this; I was just glad that we wouldn't be separated. In fact, my whole attitude toward overseas duty changed. Before, I had been annoyed at having to travel halfway around the world for the same thankless tasks I felt I could have done just as well from Langley (the one exception being my trip to Europe, where I acquired a taste for the local beer). Now that I could travel and still be with Jihi, I was up for it again.

As the summer turned to fall, we returned to Falcon House for further briefings, each time venturing a little deeper inside the labyrinth of corridors with its overlapping layers of security. Our colleagues told us the basic contours of what we were expected to do. We would be based in Wolf, a big city in a US-allied country not far from Falcon. It would be safer for us that way, they said. It would also enable us to work on potential targets outside Falcon, who might be less security-conscious than those inside, just as Jihi had done with another hard target, Badger. From there, we would be responsible for coming up with a new operational strategy to fill critical intelligence gaps and build a network of contacts who could help us understand what Falcon was doing now and what its future plans might be.

At the same time, we were explicitly *not* being transferred into Falcon House. We were yokels and interlopers, not worthy of joining the elite. That meant there were hard limits to our access. Oftentimes, we would come up against a case that was referred to in our assigned material but wasn't available. We would ask to see it and get a flat no. Or, more often, Falcon House management would tell us, "We will review the record for you." This was just "no" with extra steps, because inevitably, we would be told that it wasn't relevant to what we were doing. When we asked why, they would say, "You'll just have to trust me." I wondered whether this practice of taking things on trust hadn't contributed to the possible compromise in the first place.

It was all depressingly similar to Jihi's training rotation in the same place: secretive, whispery, exclusionary. Which begged the question: If they were so smart, why were they sending *us* to do this job, instead of someone from Falcon House who had dedicated their life and career to understanding Falcon?

Even with our limited access, we could feel the tension building inside Falcon House. From more junior people, closer to our own level, we would hear whispered details of liaison reports and speculation on what the fallout might be if Falcon House really was compromised.

Senior leaders acted like trained stoics and didn't say a word to confirm or deny this lower-level scuttlebutt. And the mid-career experts in-between waffled between being excited for the juicy gossip and anxious about internal investigations. It was clear that the whole division was close to panic mode.

CIA officers are trained to stick to established facts. Internally, the kind of chatter we heard from the rank and file is called RUMINT: rumor intelligence. Officially, you can't give it any credit. But when you are starved for information, you take what you can get.

By the early fall, we were almost ready to rock. Jihi was a couple of weeks from deploying and I was about to head into additional training to finish my SOO certification. Then, out of the blue, we were called back to door NCC-1701 for yet another meeting with Falcon House's No. 2. *Why?* we wondered. Surely after all this hard work they weren't going to pull the rug out from under us again. Then again, stranger things had happened.

This time, the meeting was in one of the executive conference rooms in Falcon House. It wasn't as deep in the labyrinth as we had been for some of our preparation, but as we walked in we could see that the walls were soundproofed and the door twice as thick as a normal door. It was a secure room in a secure department in a secure building in a secure compound. This was where they told you the secrets. We walked in and shut the double-thick door behind us.

Inside, three men were sitting around a conference table topped with black glass. No. 2 was there. So was Falcon House's chief of operations. By now, these had become familiar faces. The third face was less well known to us. A skinny old dude with a beak nose. His gray polyester suit hung off his hunched shoulders, making him look like a heron or a starving vulture. This was the chief of Falcon House's counterintelligence element: in other words, its head molehunter.

*What was this? Were they about to accuse us of something?*

No. 2 welcomed us and handed over to the counterintelligence guy, who spoke in the roundabout way that is common among spook-spotters.

"We have encountered certain complications with regard to counter-intelligence as it relates to your upcoming deployment."

"There has been a breach," said No. 2, translating for his colleague. "We suspect human penetration."

That made things clear. "Human penetration" is intelligence-speak for a mole.

*A mole?* In Falcon House, the best of the best? Our respect for Falcon intelligence, already high, now went through the roof. But we also understood, finally, the gravity of the situation.

A mole inside any of CIA's houses was a threat not only to US intelligence assets in those parts of the world, but to the entire national security of the United States. By disrupting, falsifying, or simply stopping the flow of intelligence, a mole could blind our country to the activities of a dangerous rival. Imagine two gladiators in the arena. Warily they circle each other, neither daring to attack. Then, out of the blue, one kicks sand in the other's eye and is tempted to strike while his opponent is weakened. For the blinded gladiator, meanwhile, the incentive is to lash out in self-defense. In much the same way, America's sudden inability to predict its competitor's next move increased tenfold the chances of a confrontation.

One name immediately popped into both of our minds: Aldrich Ames. Every recruit learns about him in training. In the 1980s and 1990s, Ames was a high-ranking official in CIA. Starting in 1985, Ames became a mole for a hostile foreign country and betrayed dozens of colleagues, with dire consequences. The intelligence gap continued for over a decade before Ames was finally unmasked. Reforms prompted by that fiasco were supposed to have lessened the threat. But now, more than twenty years after the end of the Cold War, it seemed something eerily similar might be brewing again.

We also knew how horrible it would be at Langley with a mole hunt going on. There would be universal suspicion, backbiting, allegations, counter-allegations. Our every move would be watched. If we started getting salad instead of soup for lunch, someone would see it as a sign. Yet Falcon House's top brass had just out and told us about the mole hunt, which was unusual. Was that a sign of trust? Or was it a warning?

The counterintelligence guy scrutinized us with his beady eyes, as if trying to catch us in an untruth.

"So are you pulling us off the assignment?" I asked, thinking that Jihi and I were about to be separated again, so soon after getting married.

"No, no, no," said the chief of operations. "Your deployment is still a go."

"We just thought you should be aware," said No. 2. "Look, we realize that this task will not be easy. So let me reassure you: you have the full support of Falcon House to tackle it however you see fit."

At that, we sat up. In Agency parlance, "full support" is code for "free rein." Translation: They were giving us permission—hell, they were even *encouraging* us—to try something new. This assignment suddenly became a great deal more interesting.

"To be clear," said the counterintelligence chief, "you are not to share this information with anyone."

Now it all made sense. We knew why the leaders of Falcon House had called on us, of all people. It wasn't for our operational brilliance. It was because we were outsiders. If the brass thought there might be a mole inside Falcon House, they wouldn't want potential suspects deployed on the other side of the world. In fact, they would want to keep as many Falcon House people as possible at headquarters, where they could more easily be monitored. Keep your friends close and your enemies closer, as the saying goes. They felt comfortable telling us precisely because we were *not* part of their club: we were not above suspicion, we were beneath it.

Besides, it was precisely because of its usual methods that Falcon House had gotten its fingers burned. It was time to try something different; and a husband-and-wife targeter-SOO combination certainly was that. Maybe my reputation for out-of-the-box ideas had reached the ears of Falcon House.

If we succeeded, America would gain a crucial edge. If we failed, well: as Falcon House made clear to us time and again, we weren't important to them anyhow. No doubt we were not the only B-team being given the same briefing. In desperation, Falcon House was likely throwing a whole bowl of spaghetti at the wall and hoping, against the odds, that a few strands might stick.

Knowing all this, did we want the job? That was the million-dollar question.

When we needed to have confidential conversations at home, we would get in the shower together. Not because it's sexy (although that's an added benefit), but because showers are harder to bug: steam drains battery life, water corrupts memory chips, and shower noise makes listening devices useless.

As the droplets drummed on our bodies, we agreed to air our biggest fears.

Jihi said, "What if we fail?"

I had to stop myself from laughing. *Of* course *we were going to fail,* I thought. Putting us up against the might and sophistication of Falcon intelligence would be like putting a T-ball batter opposite a Major League pitcher. It was an impossible task. We were *destined* to fail. We were *supposed* to fail. At the same time, I understood Jihi's concern. Her career was flourishing, unlike mine, and she worried about how it would look on her record.

I had another concern on my mind.

"What if we get killed?" I said. We knew that the Falcon security forces were not kind to spies. We were also pretty sure that they had planted a mole inside CIA, worsening our risk of being captured. We would spend the rest of our lives rotting away in a forced-labor camp, becoming brain-dead living skeletons. CIA, per protocol, would deny all knowledge of our activities, leaving us there.

"Hypothetically," Jihi said, "what if we were to —"

"Turn it down?"

"Could we do that? Hypothetically?"

Technically, we could have turned it down. But a refusal like that really would have tanked Jihi's career. More fundamentally, it's not often, even as a CIA officer, that you get the opportunity to change the course of history. If, somehow, we did succeed in recruiting new eyes and ears on the ground for America, we would be doing just that. Our careers would be made. It might even redeem my failure on the Farm. "Once in a lifetime" was the phrase we kept saying. But in most people's lifetimes, they don't get even a single opportunity to do anything remotely as significant. This was once in a million lifetimes.

"So. We're really going to do this?"

"Impossible tasks," I said, "are in my wheelhouse."

We shut off the shower. We had work to do.

# PART VI
## WOLF

## JIHI

Walking into the Agency's clandestine facility in Wolf, the friendly city that was to be our base of operations for the foreseeable future, you wouldn't know it was anything but a normal office building. You would have no way of telling that the windows were bulletproof, for example; nor that the elevator could be sealed from the outside at the flick of a switch. Coming in off the street, with the smells of fresh fruit and stale exhaust lingering in your nostrils, you wouldn't see the security contractors hiding out behind that nondescript door off the lobby. But they were there, ready to go. The place was a fortress.

I was sent out in October, while Andy stayed behind in the US to complete his final SOO certification. I spent my first two months in Wolf doing what targeters mostly do: hunting terrorists. Targeting was still a new profession within the industry, and the practice of sending us out into the field was newer still—with all the growing pains that you might expect. In local offices, we were treated as jacks of all trades, pulled into cases as needed and just as quickly forgotten about.

Early on in my time in Wolf, Mark, the office's second-in-command, showed up at my desk. Mark used to work against Badger, the hard target I had pursued during my time at Langley.

"Hey Jihi, would you do me a favor? I want to talk to this guy." He mentioned the name of a high-ranking Badger diplomat. "We were in touch a few years ago. He just got posted to Wolf. Can you get me his contact information?"

"Of course." I added it midway down my mental to-do list.

"Great. I'm just headed to the bathroom and then I'm heading out. I want to call him on my way. So if you could have that in about sixty seconds, that'd be great."

One mad scramble through the databases later, I had the info. "Great work," Mark said. "He'll be tickled to hear from me. Ciao!"

Some targeters might have felt used. Not me. I actually enjoyed working this way. I was eager to please and keen to prove myself. I liked the challenge and the faster pace. It was refreshing to be asked for information and then see my boss's boss use it right away: so different from sending a cable and then waiting around, not knowing when or whether it would be read. I developed a kind of mind meld with Mark, so that by the time he showed up to ask for some obscure piece of information, I would already have it ready for him on a Post-It note.

In December, Andy finally arrived, just in time for us to spend Christmas together. On his second day in the country, we went together so that he could introduce himself to Annika, the third-in-command at the Wolf office. We had our assignment from Falcon House, but to get any resources allocated to us locally, we would need Annika's blessing.

With her good looks and badass demeanor, Annika reminded me of Seven of Nine, the tough ex-Borg officer from *Star Trek: Voyager*. Plus, I could have sworn that, like Seven, she was part robot. She invariably wore towering spike heels, and if you heard those things clomping down the hallway, you'd better stop your conversation about the NFL or *Desperate Housewives* and get the hell back to work.

Annika was a woman of few words. Up to that point, the longest conversation I'd had with her was when she appeared in my office less than a week after I arrived.

"I need you to find me a terrorist," she'd said.

"Okay."

"I have a new case officer." She mentioned their name. "They need somebody to start working on."

I pulled out my trusty notebook. "Okay, so tell me exactly what you—"

But she was gone, leaving me to interpret her request: I had to find a source associated with terrorism, based in Wolf, who seemed like a good fit with the new case officer. No biggie.

Two weeks later, after busting my behind combing through my databases, I found a dude who seemed to tick all the boxes: a local gem dealer suspected of laundering money through his business. I began working with the case officer to get under the guy's skin.

I thought that was pretty impressive. But I never heard anything more about it from Annika. After a while, I mentioned it to my office mate, Leah, who had been there longer.

"Annika doesn't do praise," she said. "If you're not hearing from her, that means you're doing a good job."

"Oh. I see."

"If you *do* hear from her, that's when you have to start worrying."

Andy was still jet-lagged when we went in to see Annika. She swiveled her chair about five degrees away from her screen and clasped her hands, signaling for Andy to begin. He spoke about his experience in counterterrorism work, which was the Wolf office's top priority at the time. As Annika grilled him about his cases, you could see her figuring out how Andy could be of use to her.

Toward the end of his spiel, Andy added, "And now we're excited to be here, as part of a new initiative to collect against—"

"Yes. I know. I got the cable." Annika's face was a stone mask. "There's one case officer here who handles Falcon. If you want to talk about that, go talk to James." She swiveled her chair back to face her screen and zoned us out of her world.

"I just wanted to say that..." But it was clear that Annika was done with us.

I patted Andy on the leg. Time to go.

"Yes," he said. "All right. Thank you for your time."

I understood why Annika would be uninterested in Falcon, even annoyed. Wolf was a big office, and it prided itself on generating a lot of hard intelligence. Against a target like Falcon, as I knew from experience, hard intelligence would come about as easily as blood from a stone. Annika thought I was a useful resource, at least if Leah was right in her assertion that no news was good news. With his background, she probably thought Andy could be useful to her, too. And yet here we were, proposing to waste our time on this wild goose chase against the hardest of targets, without any of the proper Falcon House credentials. Above all, what Annika heard was that Andy would not only be less available to work on productive cases; he was also proposing to rob her of a good targeter. No wonder she was pissed off.

We talked to James, the Falcon House case officer Annika mentioned. He turned out to be five foot six and as all-American as they come, with a bold, infectious laugh. When he joined the Agency, he and his wife left behind promising careers in investment banking, so a sense of humor was pretty much a survival skill. James had come up through Falcon House, but at the Wolf office he was at best an oddball, at worst somebody whose painstaking work against difficult Falcon targets was bringing the whole office's productivity down. So he was delighted at last to meet two people who had been assigned the same tough gig. Besides, James was a natural at rapport-building—something you see a lot in long-serving case officers. We hit it off instantly, bonding over local beers in the office—the only place we could securely talk shop.

Andy updated us on the latest scuttlebutt from Langley. The RUMINT was not good: Falcon House was on full alert and the demand for new intel, new sources, and new insights was at a historic high.

"Tell me about it," James said. "My roster is getting squeezed from every angle."

Meanwhile, Andy said, the mole hunt was underway, and nobody was above suspicion.

"Thank God we're out here and not back there," I said. I knew how nasty mole hunts could get, with accusations and counter-accusations flying. In the 1980s and 1990s, the Agency had practically torn itself apart with such investigations.

"Amen to that," said Andy. "But don't forget, we're the poor bastards who have to put Humpty Dumpty back together again."

There was a long pause. The air conditioning vent chittered softly as it cooled what was left of my takeout (one of the first things I had discovered upon arriving in Wolf was the alley behind the office, where all manner of food stands would set up at lunchtime).

James took a deep breath. He put down his beer bottle and leaned in toward us. "You know what I really want to do?" he said. "I want to walk right up to the highest-ranking Falcon dude I can find and say, 'Hey! Wanna help America?' And if that guy says no, I'll say, 'Fair enough, sir, thank you for your time,' and move on to the next guy."

James laughed, and despite the impossible task weighing down on us, we couldn't help laughing along with him. He was the kind of guy who always made you feel as if you were in on the joke.

"I mean, I wouldn't actually do *that*. But what I'm saying is, I want to think outside the box. I want to be bold for once!"

"So why don't you?" I asked.

"Oh, you know Falcon House and its rules. We'd never get permission to do radical shit against Falcon."

Andy and I looked at each other. "Funny you should say that, dude."

"Why's that?"

A grin spread across Andy's face. "Guess who just got permission."

## ANDY

Meeting James was a turning point for me. The guy was so optimistic that I began to think we might actually be able to pull off our impossible task. On a more practical level, he was an insider with Falcon House, unlike ourselves. He could get information we couldn't.

It was also the point when I started to feel good again about my own abilities. A few conversations into our relationship, we were chatting about the money-laundering shopkeeper I had spoken to a few years before.

"Wait a minute," said James. "Aren't you a SOO? How'd they let you in front of that guy?"

I told him that I'd finished case officer training. At the mention of the Farm, James almost jumped out of his skin.

"You're a Farm graduate?"

"Well, technically, I guess. But I wasn't certified."

"No, no, no. You finished the Farm. You got the same training as me."

Had he not heard what I said? I repeated that I didn't get certified.

James waved his hand in dismissal. "That's just a piece of paper some old man gives you. If you finished the Farm, you got the skills. Dude! We need to get you out in the field."

I didn't know what "out in the field" meant—yet. But here was James, this experienced Falcon House case officer whom I respected, telling me I was a valued resource. Until that point, I had assumed that my time in Wolf was going to be just like my time at Langley, dominated by admin and logistics. But now a whole new vista of possibility opened up.

Meanwhile, Langley's demand for reports from inside Falcon was growing more desperate every day. No one really knew the damage the mole might be doing. But one of the first things every CIA officer learns is the history of devastation previous moles have caused. Aldrich Ames was a CIA mole during the Cold War whose treachery resulted in the murder of multiple foreign assets and the arrest of CIA officers abroad. Robert Hanssen, a mole inside the FBI in the '80s and '90s, compromised decades' worth of human and technical operations and destroyed a complex network of double agents.

The mole was a ticking time bomb. RUMINT and wild theories were growing by the day. We were never sure what to believe, so we chose to stay laser-focused on building our new stable of HUMINT reporters against Falcon.

While all this was going on, James received a distress message from a Falcon source. (Obviously, we can't use this source's real name, or even his real code name. So, instead, we will call this particular source by an invented cryptonym, Evade.)

Evade was a high-ranking Falcon official who had been passing secrets to the United States for some time. His message came in code, but the meaning was clear. Evade wanted an emergency meeting. Now.

James was planning to go in and meet Evade. We all knew the risks involved. In basic training, the Agency teaches you about officers who are lured into hostile territory by fake emergency meeting requests, only to be captured, tortured, held in prison for decades. So James and I worked together to plan the mission. Our idea was to have Evade tell his colleagues he was taking a vacation with his wife and family. They would charter a small riverboat and sail it deep into a forest near the border. There, James would be waiting, posing as a lepidopterist — a researcher who studies moths.

James put together a handful of what in espionage circles is called pocket litter. During World War II, pocket litter was created for a British deception op called Operation Mincemeat: letters from family, ticket stubs, bills, and receipts. Ever since, it's become a hallmark of professional intelligence operations. With his lepidopterist story and matching pocket litter at the ready, James headed to Falcon. For the duration of his trip, he entered radio silence. That much was standard procedure: on such a sensitive and dangerous mission, there must be nothing to connect him back to the Agency. What was not standard was how long he spent away. Days turned into weeks.

I did my best to keep busy. I cased locations in Wolf where James had told us targets could be found. I sought out places to meet the sources we hoped to develop. I worked on sweet-talking Annika into letting Jihi spend more of her time chasing Falcon targets.

I tried not to dwell on recent reports out of Falcon prisons, according to which espionage suspects were deliberately deprived of vitamin C so that they would contract scurvy, a condition that causes bleeding gums, anemia, and constant torturous pain in every joint. We tried to forget the forced, televised "confessions" that often followed, with foreign prisoners drugged, shackled, and visibly on the verge of unconsciousness. Some of them, their minds scrambled by relentless torture, were even induced to profess allegiance to Falcon. We tried not to imagine James in that state. Better that he had died.

## JIHI

I tried to focus on my work. I built targeting dossiers on local Falconers I suspected of being connected with their home country's intelligence services. I scoured the diplomatic lists, looking for more persons of interest. Most significantly for our future endeavors, I introduced myself to a local partner agency in the country where Wolf is situated — an agency we will call Titan — and offered to help scour through their data. Wolf's country is a US ally and Titan often cooperated with the United States on anti-terror issues.

After a full month out of pocket, James finally stumbled back into the office in Wolf, looking gaunt and underfed. For weeks, he had squatted in the forest, being eaten alive by bugs and getting sick from the food. His lepidopterist cover story was growing more moth-eaten by the day, and the local villagers, whom he was paying for his accommodation, were getting dangerously curious about his true intentions. The longer he waited, the more likely it became that Evade had been persuaded into revealing the plan. If that were to happen, James knew, it wouldn't be Evade coming in the little boat. It would be a Falcon death squad.

About three weeks in, Evade arrived at dusk — alone. His wife and kid had refused to come, thinking he had gone crazy. Evade had stayed behind as long as he dared to try to persuade them, but to no avail. Finally, he decided to come on his own, despite the damage to his cover story of taking a vacation with the family.

"I can't do this anymore," Evade told James. "This is the last time."

James, dizzy and weak from food poisoning, worked hard to persuade Evade to continue his work for the United States. James managed to keep Evade in the hut with him for a few days, during which time they bonded over their shared experience of fatherhood. But it was no use. James couldn't save the case. Evade was adamant: he had to stop. Finally, James watched Evade depart on the boat.

## ANDY

Of course, we were delighted to have James back in one piece, albeit a skinnier piece than before. We celebrated in the usual way: with a late-night beer at the office. But James's mood was anything but cheerful.

"Well, that's it," he said. "That dude Evade quit. I'm done."

"You really have nobody else left?" asked Jihi.

"Well, I've got one. A guy we're calling Bridge. But see, there's a problem."

Bridge, James explained, was a military engineer working on a secret project for Falcon. Bridge was the kind of guy who had probably been quite formidable in his youth but nowadays was eating and drinking more than he exercised. As a result, he had grown rotund, while his hair had retreated to a horseshoe of gray. But he was a snappy dresser, always in a tailored suit and tie, with a nice watch on his wrist. Bridge was not from Falcon, but the military there relied on him for his specialist expertise in the field. In return, they treated him like a VIP.

Bridge's red-carpet shtick made sense: the tech that he worked on was advanced and important. The trouble was, Falcon had stolen it from the United States. Nothing Bridge could say about it would be news to the US government. As far as the Agency's management was concerned, Bridge was an intelligence black hole.

"Annika's telling me to dump him. Langley says the same thing. And you know what? I can see where they're coming from."

Granted, perhaps James's interest in continuing his relationship with Bridge wasn't all about business. Working for Falcon had made Bridge a rich man, and he liked to spend that wealth on swanky resorts, treating his friends to cocktails and casino chips. For James, the end of Bridge would mean the end of those good times.

It seemed to me there was nothing to be done. There was no getting around it: Bridge simply didn't have any information we didn't already know.

"Oh man, I'm sorry," I said.

James and I both went quiet. Was this how our mission would end? Not with a bang but a whimper? Just when I was beginning to feel positive, it seemed as if our last chance was withering away. My beer was tasting more bitter by the mouthful.

**JIHI**

As a targeter, I saw things differently. Listening to James describing his contact, multiple bells rang in my head.

"But wait a minute," I said. "This guy Bridge must work with other people, right?"

"Well, sure."

"At least some of them military? Intelligence even?"

"I guess, but—"

I could feel the excitement building—the same bubbly energy that always took over when I made a breakthrough on a tough case.

"Remember when we got bin Laden?" I said. "It took years. But we eventually found him. You know how, right? Not through some other terrorist commander. We got to him through his courier. Just the guy who was delivering letters. How much did that courier know about what al-Qaeda was doing? Most likely next to nothing. But that wasn't the point. The point was who he was connected to. See what I'm saying?"

James thought for a moment. "I guess I don't see the equivalence. We're talking about Falcon here, not some terrorist group. It's a different level of sophistication."

"Hold that thought," I said, setting down my beer on James's desk. "Wait here."

Still giddy with excitement, I ran upstairs to my office, where I kept a bunch of enormous six-foot rolls of paper propped up in one corner. I came back clutching one of those rolls plus a single-page targeting summary I had put together.

"Look at this guy," I said, slapping the one-pager down on the table. The target was a local restaurant owner who was allowing his premises to be used after hours for extremist meetings. "If we only ask *what* he knows, it's a boring list. Like, we know how the restaurant business works, right? He's not privy to operations, personnel, logistics, any of that. By Langley's logic, he's useless as a source."

"Right," said James. He was looking confused.

"But what if we ask *who* he knows?" With a flourish of pride, I unfurled the giant roll of paper and, standing on a chair, fixed it to the wall with sticky tack. It was a spider diagram I had printed out on a huge printer we had at the office in Wolf. On the fringes of the diagram were labeled photographs of the senior leadership of an anti-US terrorist group. In the center was my corrupt restaurateur. Lines radiated out from him in all directions, connecting him to all the local extremists who frequented his establishment. Each of them, in turn, was connected to others, and on and on up the chain to the very top of the organization. Some of the links in the chain were question marks or code names, their true identities as yet unknown to the Agency. But thanks to the foodie, we knew where to focus our efforts.

"Holy shit," said James. Like most case officers back then, he had never worked closely with a targeter, meaning that he was unfamiliar with our methods. I thought back to the difficulties I had experienced communicating with case officers when I worked at Langley. It was already obvious that immediate, face-to-face conversations were way better than stilted, time-consuming email threads.

"That's not all," I said. "A restaurant owner is not going to be as security-conscious as the guys who do operations. He'll be easier to approach. Easier to get talking. In counterterrorism targeting, we go out of our way to find people like that. We call them nodes. Your guy Bridge is the same. He's not useless at all. In fact, he's the opposite of useless. You want to make use of him? Don't ask what he knows. Ask who."

James swigged his beer. His eyes traveled across my outsized spider diagram. I smiled at Andy, who winked back. If there's one thing targeters know besides databases, it's how to ram a point home with splashy visuals. In Wolf, I had perfected this art, using Microsoft Publisher to add bright colors and snappy designs to my target summaries to highlight key points about each one.

"So let me get this straight," James said at length. "Langley says this guy's hopeless. But you're here telling me to go back and let him buy me whiskey and poker chips?"

Andy and I looked at each other. "Pretty much," I said. "Yeah."

"What can I say?" James said, clinking his beer bottle with each of us. "That works for me."

Annika, predictably, was not eager to try this new method. To her, it seemed like a waste of James's talents to sic him on a source whose work was already known about. But, as we pointed out, the rest of James's network could be exposed to the mole, so what was left to lose?

"Fine," she said. "You get one more meeting with Bridge. One." If Bridge didn't start producing, it was clear that Annika would have no hesitation in pulling the plug.

So James went back to Bridge for one last hurrah, this time probing not for technical details but for gossip about his coworkers. He hit the mother lode. Bridge, it turned out, was one of nature's complainers — especially when fueled by copious casino cocktails. More specifically, he was one of those people who has never worked with anyone he didn't think was an idiot. Bridge relished the opportunity to dump on his Falcon colleagues for their alleged laziness, incompetence, and rudeness. James was only too happy to add gasoline to the fire, validating Bridge's complaints while at the same time complimenting his work and marveling at how well-connected he was.

James returned to the Wolf office and reported Bridge's disgruntled ranting to me. I started building out a new spider diagram. Bridge didn't always name names, but he let slip enough information for me to figure out who was who and start building up targeting packages. Just as I thought, it turned out that Bridge worked closely with a massive network of Falconers with ties to military and intelligence — enough to keep us busy for years.

Suddenly, Langley was very interested indeed. Even Annika was impressed enough to give James the green light to continue. So maybe the Bustamantes were not entirely full of shit.

That success got me thinking: how else could we make use of counterterrorism logic against Falcon? An idea started to take shape in my mind. Over a third round of beers in the office (our fridge was always well stocked), I made my proposal to Andy and James.

As before, my starting point was America's deceased public enemy number one. We eventually found Osama bin Laden, but it took almost a decade and the combined expertise of the US Intelligence

Community. One reason was how small a target he presented to the outside world. Just one person (the courier) linked bin Laden's Abbottabad compound to the rest of al-Qaeda. Given this bottlenecking of communication, some pundits thought that he couldn't possibly have been doing anything meaningful, besides surviving. Yet documents picked up on the raid proved that bin Laden wasn't just in hiding. Despite all the insulation around him, he was actively running al-Qaeda from his bolt-hole in Pakistan. In other words, the model worked, both operationally and security-wise. Maybe it was time for the good guys to try something similar?

Next, I reminded Andy of his own *Groundhog Day* experience working against terrorism.

"The bad guys had a pretty good MO going on there, too," I said. "Wouldn't you say?"

"That's one way of putting it."

"But you want to know the good news?"

"Sure."

"Falcon *hasn't* spent the last decade fighting terrorism the way the US has."

"Wait," said Andy. "How is that the good news? Isn't that part of how we got into this mess? We spent so much time chasing al-Qaeda that we dropped the ball on Falcon and our other adversaries."

"Look at it another way. We now know how terrorists operate. The Falconers haven't had to worry about it. Meaning that it's not something they're prepared to deal with. We've spent years battling terrorism. What if we gave Falcon a taste of that medicine?"

Realization began to dawn across James and Andy's faces.

"Oh man," said James.

"So you're saying we should..."

"That's exactly what I'm saying."

"Oh man."

I grinned. "Let's build a terrorist cell."

## ANDY

Falcon House had two weaknesses. The first was the one Jihi had encountered while working against Badger: officers typically worked in groups according to skill set. These groups had hardened into silos, making communication between them slow and stilted. That was why, for example, Jihi's spider diagram was so new to James: he had no real prior experience of working with a targeter.

The second weakness was that, above a certain level, management had access to everyone and everything. This was one reason Falcon House was so vulnerable to moles: by turning the right person, you would unlock a treasure trove of intelligence and identities, just as Falcon intelligence was doing right now with their mole.

Jihi's proposal would take that model and turn it inside out. Instead of being cogs in a clunking bureaucracy, we would create our own tight-knit, self-sufficient organization. We would bring together all the major skill sets: not just a targeter and case officers, but a linguist, a tech team, and a dedicated case manager (me) responsible for communicating with Langley, obtaining the necessary permissions and resources, and offering guidance to the case officers. We would all work out of the same building in Wolf. If we needed to communicate, there would be no forms to fill out, no ponderous back-and-forth in written cable traffic: we'd talk right away, in person. We'd get it done.

Most importantly of all, we would insulate ourselves against penetration the same way Osama bin Laden's cell had done: only one of us would ever be visible to the outside world, including Falcon House itself. And the logical candidate to be that one vulnerable person, the equivalent of bin Laden's courier, would be our case manager: me.

"My love," I said after a long pause, "you are either crazy or a genius."

"You mean I can't be both?"

"I guess we'll find out."

It didn't have a name, this new model. But just to be dramatic, let's call it the Cell.

# PART VII
# THE WHITE WHALE

## ANDY

A new batch of case officers would soon be rotating into Wolf, and the Cell wanted first dibs. We had a few requirements. First, we didn't want anyone on their very first tour: Falcon was a hard target and required some experience. Second, we couldn't take anyone who was a liaison to the local government: the Cell would need absolute secrecy. Third, they should be reasonably familiar with Falcon or at least its region.

Within those criteria, we had to take what we could get. I pitched the idea to a few case officers. Mostly, their response was a resounding, "Hell no!" I understood why. CIA may be the world's premier intelligence agency, but it's also a bureaucracy. There are annual targets to meet, and for case officers those targets revolve around turning foreign contacts into sources of intelligence. Falcon was already one of the toughest places to do that, and we were proposing to use an untested model that must have seemed a little insane. For most case officers, it would be far easier to make their quotas in other ways.

No: to want to work for the Cell, you had to be, let's say, unconventional. Kind of like me and Jihi. Luckily, among the new batch of case officers arriving in Wolf, there were a few people who fit that description.

Our first case officer recruit was a young woman we will call Tasha. Tasha was like a flower child out of Woodstock, big into chakras and healing crystals. Walking into her cube at the Wolf office was like entering a Tibetan monastery, complete with prayer flags. Tasha came with a trailing husband, Leonard, who was not in intelligence but knew what Tasha did for a living, and their son, a toddler we will call Monty. Leonard was a fun dad. In the living room of the Wolf apartment rented for them by the US government, he would put Monty in the middle of the floor with a bucket of ping-pong balls and ride his bike around in a circle so Monty could throw the balls at him. Meanwhile, Tasha stayed aloof from the chaos, gliding around like Mother Nature. At the time, we found it bewildering. But Leonard's big dad energy would later prove crucial in Tasha's most significant case.

Our other two case officers, Beverly and Luke, came as a married couple. We liked this, because it would help keep the Cell as close-knit as possible. Beverly was an imposing woman in her mid-forties, feisty, funny, loud, and persuasive. Luke was almost the opposite: quiet and low-key. You could imagine him on the campus of some liberal arts college in a tweed jacket with leather patches on the elbows. Luke was also about five years younger than Beverly—another seemingly random fact that was to prove critical in an important case.

Beverly and Luke had long since decided that climbing the career ladder was not as important as getting posted together. Previously, they had both been posted in a war zone. In Wolf, they occupied the same office, where they pulled down the cube walls and pushed their desks together so they could look at each other over the tops of their computers and play footsie under the desk. They had to make the most of whatever time they could get together, even if it was office time: as case officers in the Cell, they were going to be busy. Refreshingly uninterested in KPIs and quotas, Beverly and Luke were up for anything, especially if it sounded fun.

Just like that, the Cell grew from three people to six: me, Jihi, James, Tasha, Beverly, and Luke. Our little team had experience, but it was almost exclusively in hunting terrorists—a very different discipline from trying to recruit Falcon sources. Of the six of us, only one— James—spoke fluent Falconian. Thanks to my language exchange years ago, I had basic competence. The others had none. Could we really take on one of the world's top intelligence services? We were about to find out.

With Tasha, Beverly, and Luke on board, we all squeezed into Beverly and Luke's office and huddled around their pushed-together desks for an initial briefing. James spoke first, to get everyone pumped up; experienced case officers tend to be good at telling people what to do in a way that makes them excited to do it, and James was a master of that dark art.

"Langley has given us a free hand against Falcon," he said. "Local management here is supportive. Chances like this don't come around too often, trust me. So let's get out there."

I then spoke about the mission. "We are looking for a few different kinds of people," I said. "Government officials would be great. But also executives in companies with strong ties to the Falcon government: natural resources, military engineering, construction. Ultimately, we'd like to target intelligence officers, assuming we can get to them. The dream scenario would be to make our own mole inside Falcon intelligence."

Our case officers smiled and nodded around the table. Everyone knew how tough an ask that was—but also what a coup it would be, if we pulled it off.

"We will start here in Wolf and network our way into Falcon," I said. "They'll be less guarded here. But remember, these are Falconers we are talking about. They will be wary of any direct questions about their professional lives. Better to approach them from a personal angle to begin with, even if you meet them in a professional setting. So don't ask about their jobs. Ask about their kids. Ask what they do for fun."

My little speech focused on people, not secrets, and there was a good reason for that. It's important to note here that real-life intelligence officers are almost never tasked with discovering one particular secret, the way James Bond might be sent specifically to find out Blofeld's latest dastardly plan to take over the world. Reality is not that clear-cut. Instead, you pull a list of general collection priorities from the National Intelligence Strategy published by the Director of National Intelligence every year. In the case of Falcon at that time (and even more so now), that list was as long as your arm. It was making invasion threats against its neighbors. Developing new weaponry, like the secret project Bridge was working on. Carrying out offensive technological operations. And now, apparently, making moles inside CIA itself.

With those priorities in hand, the intelligence officer's task is to find someone—anyone—who might be able to share any information about the items on that list. Once again, you take what you can get, especially against a hard target, where you can expect the immediate brush-off from nine out of ten people you approach. However, in the Cell, the process would be less scattershot, because we would be working hand-in-glove with our targeter.

**JIHI**

That was my cue. I unveiled another spider diagram, this time featuring the network I was in the process of unearthing around Bridge,

James's supposedly useless third-country military engineer. You could practically see light bulbs flashing over the heads of our new case officers. I described my role as matchmaking: out of the data I had, I would find targets and targeting opportunities. Then I would take charge of assigning the most appropriate case officer to each one. This was going to be an interesting ride.

After that first briefing, things really started to pop for the Cell. Scouring a list I had of Falcon diplomats in Wolf, I found somebody who might be of interest: a senior official we will call Zefram. In his late forties or early fifties, Zefram cut a more impressive figure than the average rumple-suited government worker. He was lean and polished. Well groomed, he was never seen without a collared shirt, and rarely without a tie. His wardrobe seemed to range from business casual all the way to business business. I called Langley and asked them to run a trace on his true name. It turned out that somebody—multiple people, in fact—had flagged him as potentially being a high-ranking Falcon intelligence officer. But besides that, there was not much in his file, and that absence intrigued me.

I had Langley contact CIA's peer agencies in the US Intelligence Community—the NSA, the military intelligence agencies, and so on—to see what they might have on Zefram. It was the same story from each of them: a lot of flags, very little concrete information. What we did get were theories. One theory said that he was the regional chair of Falcon intelligence. Another claimed that he was the Falcon leader's personal representative in Wolf. Either way, he was beginning to look like a dream target.

I started building a targeting package on Zefram. The ultimate objective, as always, was the bump—the natural-seeming approach—followed by a blossoming relationship in which we would find ways to make ourselves useful to him. If Zefram was who we thought he was, he would be wary of foreigners, especially Americans. We would need a subtle method. I knew from experience that such a potentially valuable target would be a good candidate for surveillance.

If we were to target Zefram for surveillance, we would need to call in an expert. As luck would have it, an officer with this specialty was in the region and was talked into visiting Wolf to discuss this potential operation in person. He arrived with a case full of gadgets that looked like he had just cleared out a cyberpunk junk shop. As he unpacked, nearly every surface was festooned with lots of fun stuff we can't talk about. To this *Star Trek* nerd, it felt like being inside a Borg Cube.

This officer, Will, defied the hacker stereotype. He was in his twenties, immaculately dressed and styled. He loved to party and could charm a lady as easily as he could do intel work. Don't tell Andy, but I had a little crush on him.

I described the Cell to Will. He got it immediately, and he wanted in. He was especially excited to be invited to deploy against Falcon. Because here is another way it's not like the movies: tech operations are not used nearly as much as you would think. Intelligence gathering is still dominated by human sources, and that's especially true when it comes to hard targets like Falcon, which guard ruthlessly against any technological vulnerability.

I asked Will to describe his capabilities, waving a hand at the doo-hickeys lined up on the table. What could he do with all this stuff?

Will shook his head. "I don't work that way. If you need information, just ask. My team and I will figure out how to get it for you."

So I told him what we knew about Zefram and what we wanted to know. First off, as usual, I was looking for a pattern of life. Where did Zefram go during the workday, and at what times? What car did he use? Did he go out at night? If so, where? And so on.

Together, Will and I hashed out the details of a surveillance package, triangulating our needs with the available resources. We settled on an initial period of two weeks, during which we would monitor Zefram from 7 a.m. to 11 p.m. (at his age, we figured he wouldn't be out later than that, and now that I am approaching that age myself, I can confirm that we were correct in that assumption).

The centerpiece of our plan was a surveillance spot adjacent to Zefram's home. Air conditioning would have interfered with the surveillance, so Will had to sit there for hours in sweltering heat. But his suffering soon paid off.

The result of Will's efforts was hundreds of hours' worth of information, almost all of it in Falconian. But only one member of our team, James, spoke that language fluently. We would need a linguist to translate all that information for us, and I had just the woman for the job.

In Wolf, as in other cities around the world where the United States maintains a presence, most American officials live in regular apartments leased by the US government. Our apartment in Wolf was in a big complex that was also home to several other Americans. (You could always tell the US-rented apartments: they were the ones with the reinforced steel doors.) Right after I arrived in Wolf, a new neighbor had moved into another apartment in our complex: Dianna, the kickass interpreter I had worked with when debriefing the military commander from Badger.

Dianna spoke several languages, including Falconian, well enough to translate accurately under any circumstances. When Will came back with a load of information, Dianna would often stay up all night translating it. She and I would discuss the results over rounds of her notorious butter cake.

To begin with, we got nothing but junk: groceries, fights between Zefram and his wife, talks about his son's school homework, and all the other normal stuff that happens in any household. When he did talk about work, it was all consistent with his diplomatic cover. Clearly, we were dealing with a meticulous individual.

The really telling revelation, however, came from our surveillance of Zefram's daily routine. Long story short, he didn't have one. He traveled to and from the Falcon embassy, but at different times each day and using different vehicles. He had a whole pool of cars and drivers on call, and he would mix and match them seemingly at random. The routes they would take through the city varied, too. Aside from that, he rarely went out, and never on a regular schedule. When he did leave the house, he would have one driver take him to the location and another pick him up when he was done, even if the errand was a short one. Once or twice, he visited a particular bathhouse in the city. He went to a few stores, including an unusual number of different pharmacies, which struck me as odd—I filed that information away for possible future use.

Back at our office, we built a map of Zefram's movements over the two weeks during which we watched him. It looked like a bowl of spaghetti, just noodles all jumbled. Zefram's pattern of life, in other words, was practically nonexistent. We knew from experience and training how difficult it would be to live without a pattern of life, and how painstaking you would have to be to pull it off. Yet here was Zefram doing it.

We had surveilled him for fourteen days and had nothing to show for it. But this is one of those moments when the logic of intelligence work goes topsy-turvy. Any normal person would have shown us something, anything, approximating a routine. Zefram seemed to have none, and that spoke volumes about his importance. Even with a hard target like Falcon, it's rare to find an individual so heavily defended. From this, we concluded that Zefram must be working on something really, really clandestine. And that, of course, only made us more determined to make contact with him.

Zefram was going to be our white whale. Chasing him down would take every bit of the creativity and patience I had cultivated while working against Badger, plus more than a little luck.

In the meantime, we'd need smaller fish to keep us going.

## ANDY

Collecting human intelligence can be kind of like dating in your thirties. Your real agenda might be to find a life partner to have kids with before it's too late. To you, this agenda is both important and urgent. But you can't bring it up on a first date. In fact, you have to be pretty deep into the relationship before you can even start to talk about marriage and kids directly. In the same way, and for obvious reasons, you can't just say to a new contact, "Uncle Sam's gotta know about these new missiles you're building. Tell me everything!"

Instead, we take the softly-softly approach, part of a widely known CIA framework for agent recruitment. Phase one is getting the target's attention. Maybe you start shopping at the same corner store. For weeks or months, you don't interact. You just let them see that you are a fellow customer. Nothing weird about that. Then one day you both reach for the same bag of Swedish Fish. "Oh," you say, "are you as addicted to these things as I am? I've loved them since I was a kid and I can't quit!" And now, boom, you're bonding over Swedish Fish. It's the espionage equivalent of the meet-cute in a rom-com.

Phase two is to show them how you might be able to assist each other. Maybe it just so happens that we are in the same industry or enjoy shared extracurricular activities. Typically this comes as a "no kidding" moment: "Wait, you also play pétanque / love Zeffirelli movies / work in rivet manufacturing? What are the odds?!" The best version of this comes when you can be both useful and fun to be around: for example, maybe you are both a source of business contacts and a fun drinking buddy.

Phase three is friendship. And here is another thing to note. Most of the time, the relationships between our case officers and their Falcon contacts are genuine—not fake or transactional. Partly, this is just the American style of intelligence gathering, in distinction to that of our rivals (and even some of our allies), whose collection methods can get brutal much more readily. But it also comes of necessity.

In some parts of the world, it might be possible to form an instant friendship: "You like scotch? I like scotch! Let's drink together, my friend!"

Citizens of Falcon are not like that. They are extremely well attuned to whom they can and cannot trust; when you live in an unfree society with blanket surveillance, knowing who will and who won't report you for talking smack about the leadership is a literal matter of life and death. So it's essential to earn their confidence—and in order to do that, you have to be genuine with them on at least a social level. When CIA case officers make contact with a Falcon target especially, they are seeking to strike up a real friendship, not just manipulate their source.

Once a relationship is firmly established, you might start finding ways of making it more confidential: more secluded meetings, and so on. Only then do we reach the final phase: admitting to your contact that, in addition to being their friend, you are an intelligence officer. Naturally, you only do that once you are pretty damn sure they are willing to become a formal, cooperating US intelligence asset.

Obviously, this painstaking process takes time: in most cases involving citizens of Falcon, many years. And sometimes, in intelligence as in dating, you find out that all this time you've been kissing a frog.

## JIHI

The classic way that case officers meet potential contacts is the same way anyone does: by networking. They go to parties, conferences, trade fairs, anywhere people collect business cards. Then they pursue whoever seems interesting.

Tasha, our resident hippie, was posing as an executive. So when I found out that a big conference was taking place nearby, she was a natural fit to attend.

It was there that she met Justice, a female executive in the stone-quarrying business. Justice was a Falconer, but based in Wolf. Like Zefram, Justice was a power dresser, always in sharp suits. She also wore a lot of designer perfume, which Tasha, more attuned to patchouli and coconut oil, found irritating. Justice was constantly, frenetically busy on her phone: the very image of a go-getter.

Why might she be an attractive contact? With Falcon undergoing a huge force buildup, Justice's company might well be supplying military infrastructure projects: installations, bases, factories. If she didn't know anything about that directly, her network of contacts might. In Falcon, the distinction between business and government, particularly in a key sector like infrastructure, is not as clear-cut as it is in the United States. For all we knew, Justice could have been a second Bridge, with a spider diagram of her own.

Plus, it was unusual to find a woman in such a male-dominated sector. Maybe she and Tasha could bond over that. Justice was only in her thirties, not much older than Tasha. Guided by me, Andy, and James, Tasha built a relationship with Justice over a string of girls' nights out: happy hours, dinners, visits to the nail bar. The last of these was particularly amusing: as an earth-mother hippie, Tasha didn't get her nails done—in fact, she barely had any nails to speak of—but these outings were crafted to please Justice, not Tasha.

Justice turned out to be corrupt as hell, bragging to Tasha about how she would scam clients by supplying them with substandard stone. This openness encouraged Tasha: apparently, Justice didn't hold anything back. She talked a big game, too, dropping names left and right. According to her, she was always the preferred bidder for this or that government project, in touch with this or that person, and so on.

When Tasha returned from her shenanigans with Justice, I would run the information she had collected through the databases available to me. Nothing remotely interesting came back. In parallel, I ran open-source searches on her business and found out that she had opened and wound up four companies in the past five years. Most of the contracts she said she had won were outright fabrications. It became clear why Justice was so eager to talk to Tasha: she was hustling to keep her business afloat. Unfortunately, Justice had nothing to offer in return, other than bluster.

Having worked so hard to persuade the higher-ups that Bridge was worth pursuing, it was galling to have to turn around and tell a fellow Cell member to break it off with a target whom she hoped would be the next big super-connector. James was the best-liked member of the Cell, so I enlisted his help to lead the intervention.

Tasha listened, visibly bummed out by the bad news. As a young woman in a world run by old men, she struggled to get anyone to talk to her. At a trade fair, at least one potential contact had literally run in the opposite direction when she tried to strike up conversation, spooked by her age, gender, and nationality.

"Look," James said. "You're worth more than this. Your skills are better deployed elsewhere."

Tasha threw up her hands. "What should I do?" she said. "I don't have any other targets."

"I know," said James. "But Jihi is so good at her job, she'll find you someone else to make contact with, I'm sure."

I nodded along, hoping Tasha wouldn't see from my expression just how tall an order this would be.

Of course, none of us was happy that Justice turned out to be a dud. But on the other hand, the cell model had helped us reach that conclusion much faster than we would have under traditional methods. Usually, case officers sat with other case officers—people who are paid to be persistent. They would have egged Tasha on. "Give it time," they would say. "Keep working at it. You'll get something out of her one of these days, you'll see."

Andy and I, as the Cell's targeter and case manager, respectively, were able to take a different perspective. Because we worked with Tasha every day, we knew the Justice case inside and out. At the same time, because we had more distance from the case than she did, we were able to see that Tasha was on the road to nowhere. So in a roundabout way, the Cell's structure was already proving its worth.

Meanwhile, the Cell's very first contact continued to pay dividends. While we were still getting set up, James continued his friendship with Bridge, lending an empathetic ear to his whining about his colleagues and in the process learning all about the network of people he worked with.

Out of Bridge's gossiping and whining to James, I extracted thirty or so of the juicier-sounding names—mostly Falcon officials and those known to have been in touch with them—and cross-referenced them with other databases I had on hand. One in particular stood out. Bridge said he had done some consulting work on the side for a company in the construction business with ties to the Falcon government. He dropped the name of its CEO, a man we will call Kingpin.

This was interesting. Given the nature of Bridge's work as a military engineer (remember, James initially made contact with him hoping to find out more about his work on his secret project), this presumably meant that Kingpin's company was doing more interesting stuff than it seemed from the outside. That made sense. If Falcon needed to build a new military base or intelligence facility, Kingpin was exactly the kind of guy they would tap. Better yet, Kingpin was based outside of Falcon, albeit not in Wolf.

How to approach him? Tasha, of course, would be a natural fit. Unfortunately, Kingpin was a man and significantly older — both major handicaps in a culture that values age and Y chromosomes. He was also out of Tasha's league in terms of his wealth: he was a CEO, after all, and he looked the part, wearing handmade Italian suits and tooling around in his Maserati. So at first, it seemed like we might have trouble orchestrating a successful bump. But I kept an eye on Kingpin's movements around the region, just in case. That was how I eventually spotted an opening for Tasha.

Since it was good news this time, I decided to tell Tasha myself. I guess that's one of the perks of being a matchmaker. When she arrived in my office, I handed her a dossier on Kingpin, including his biography, his photo, his general schedule, his level of access, and so on. I also included whatever details I was able to glean about Kingpin's family members. I learned that Kingpin's wife, like him, spoke good English and held a college degree, which probably meant that Kingpin had a more enlightened view of women than a lot of wealthy Falcon men — and that Mrs. Kingpin likely held more sway in the household than your average Falcon woman.

"Okay," Tasha said. "Interesting."

"Plus, he has a son who's only a little older than Monty."

"Okay."

"There's more." I smiled. "We found out where he's going to be next week. I'll give you a clue: it's not a conference." I slid another document across the table, glossier than the previous one. It was a brochure for a beach resort: king-size beds, private beach, oceanfront spa. "Remember what Andy said about approaching people from a personal angle? He's traveling with his wife and their son."

"Ooh." Tasha's eyes widened as she flipped through the gleaming pictures and perused the menu of spa treatments.

"I've booked a deluxe suite for you, Leonard, and Monty. Just a couple doors down from the target. My treat. Well, Uncle Sam's."

"Jihi, you're the best." This was about as close to James Bond as it was going to get—if 007 had a kid and spouse in tow.

Just over a week later, Tasha was checking into the resort with her family. She spent much of day one casing the joint, while acting as naturally as possible. She ate lunch slowly, hung out poolside, patrolled the grounds, even lingered for as long as she dared outside Kingpin's suite, hoping for a glimpse of the great man. At dinner, Tasha scanned the restaurant while Leonard—ever the fun dad—kept Monty entertained by making origami animals out of bits of paper. No sign of Kingpin or his family. After they put Monty to bed, Tasha went to the bar for a drink. Still no sign. Tasha grew worried. Had Kingpin left early? Had he gotten wise to the fact that he was about to be approached by an American spy? Was this contact going to be a bust, just like Justice?

The next morning, Tasha was hoping for better luck, and this time she got it: as they entered the restaurant for breakfast, she spotted Kingpin with his family. Even better: the table next to theirs was open. This was her chance.

She elbowed Leonard in the ribs and whispered, "That's the guy."

"Roger that," said Leonard. "Commencing Operation Chitchat."

They made a beeline for the open table. Midway through breakfast,

Tasha got the opening she was looking for—courtesy of Kingpin Jr. Sitting in his high chair, the toddler had a sudden meltdown and threw his utensils on the floor. A two-year-old needing to be calmed? This was a job for Leonard. He seized a napkin and began folding animals. Kingpin Jr. got curious and stopped wailing. Meanwhile, Tasha took a spare set of utensils from their table and magnanimously handed it to Kingpin.

"Kids, huh?"

"Yes," said Kingpin. "They are the same everywhere."

"Ain't that the truth."

After a bit more small talk, Tasha made a playdate for Monty and Kingpin Jr. later that day at the pool. At first, she found herself mainly speaking to Mrs. Kingpin, but Leonard was working his own brand of magic on the CEO. It was impossible not to click with Leonard—the guy was just so infectiously enthusiastic. People poured out their life stories to him. While Tasha held a giggling Monty in the water, she heard Leonard exclaiming from his poolside sun lounger.

"Oh man, you like backgammon?!" he said. "My wife loves backgammon! Hey honey, did you know he likes backgammon?"

*What are the odds?* Tasha thought wryly.

It was a textbook bump. The families promptly arranged two more playdates for Monty and Kingpin Jr., and by the end of the trip, they had exchanged phone numbers and were making plans to hang out again. Tasha had just made another breakthrough for the Cell.

## ANDY

Orchestrating Tasha's bump with Kingpin was a stroke of genius on Jihi's part. It was a kind of intelligence jiu-jitsu, turning Tasha's cultural weakness (young, female, a mother) into a strength by presenting her in the first instance not as a work contact but as a potential family friend—one who turned out to be in a similar business (small world!).

And equally important: Tasha went in with all the resources at her disposal, chatty husband and cute toddler included. In short order, our targeter found the source and conceived of the match, and our case officer executed the bump to perfection. Without the cross-functional teamwork enabled by the cell model, this likely never would have happened.

Tasha's dual relationship with Kingpin was vital. If she were only a family friend, Kingpin would likely have skipped out on future meetings, leaving her stuck with his wife and Kingpin Jr., both of whom were significantly less promising as sources of intelligence. If, on the other hand, she were only a work contact, Kingpin would have been reluctant to be seen alone with a young, American woman. He would have feared a scandal—which, in Falcon, can have dire consequences.

Since Tasha found a way to be both, connecting with Kingpin was a lot easier. The two families would get together so their sons could play. Tasha and Kingpin could talk shop on the sidelines. And talk shop they did. Unlike Justice, Kingpin proved to be exquisitely well connected within Falcon. He mentioned Falcon officials who had hired his company, and more powerful, better-connected CEOs who had subcontracted him on big projects for the Falcon government.

Tasha could be useful and fun for these folks, too, but they rarely left Falcon. Before too long, in other words, Tasha would need to head into Falcon. But another officer would need to go in ahead of her, to set things up for her meetings. That somebody was me.

# PART VIII
# GOING IN

## ANDY

Case officers working on hostile turf would act as one another's operational support. James, for example, might go into Falcon with a dual mission: First, he would meet with the government official he was developing as an intelligence source. Second, he would find time, let's say, to scout a restaurant his colleague, Jane, was considering for a meeting. In turn, Jane might bring something in for Jonathan, and so on down the line.

In the never-ending struggle for balance between convenience and security, this system won points for efficiency but also presented a potential vulnerability: if just one case officer's cover got blown, the whole chain would be compromised. In a place like Falcon, awash with sophisticated surveillance both traditional and technological, a single blown cover would put a *lot* of officers at risk.

The Cell tried to strike a balance. As the Cell's dedicated case manager, I took on the role of operational support, and that included setting things up for any Cell case officers about to brave Falcon. I was well suited to this role. I wasn't a case officer myself—my failure with

Major Bondoy had seen to that—so I wouldn't be seen as horning in on anyone's operation. But I did know all the tradecraft, including what James and Tasha would need to execute their missions properly.

It boiled down to places and property. First, I would explore potential locations for meetings and other operational acts. Second, I would buy stuff, such as gifts for case officers to give their contacts—for example, an expensive bottle of scotch that Tasha could use to woo one of Kingpin's well-heeled CEO friends—as well as useful items like various communication platforms that authoritarian governments were in the process of banning precisely because they were harder to track. The fact that I was the one making the purchases meant that the transactions were less likely to be traced back to our case officers.

Purchasing items was not suspicious in itself; but when I judged that the coast was clear, I would also procure less salubrious articles. Sometimes operations require you to think and look like your enemy. This can require procuring items of questionable legality. I can't say much more.

Finally, and least subtly, sometimes I would simply find a place inside Falcon to conceal large amounts of dollar-denominated cash, because when all else fails, a well-placed bribe can go a long way.

Clearly, I wouldn't be going into Falcon as Andy Bustamante. I had to be somebody else entirely. The need to take on a different identity is by no means confined to CIA operatives, nor are the basic methods used to achieve it. But what I'm about to describe applies, broadly speaking, to anyone from a CIA case officer spying on Falcon to an undercover cop looking to bust a drug ring. Different priorities, same basic process.

On the most basic level, I was already posing as a different person. As far as the government of Wolf's country was concerned, I was completing an overseas posting as a mid-level employee of a US federal agency we will call the Bureau of Paperwork. In intelligence and law-enforcement work, this type of cover is called "cover for status": it gave me a plausible reason to be in Wolf.

If you are going to meet a contact for intelligence purposes, on the other hand, you need a much different type of cover, one that justifies your presence in hostile territory and your meeting with that person, to the satisfaction not just of a casual observer but of a counterintelligence officer trained to hunt down spies. This is "cover for action," and it's way more complex.

Imagine you are a thief, out to burgle some rich person's house. When you're only poking around the neighborhood, you don't need much of a story to justify why you're there. Maybe you're looking at real estate to buy. Maybe you're just passing through. You're unlikely to attract much attention. Eventually, however, you need to go pick the lock on the rich person's front door. Now, if you are caught, you need a much more robust reason for doing what you are doing. Maybe you say you're installing a home-security system. Well, fine: that's your cover for action. What make and model of security system? Where will you install the sensors? How long have you been installing home-security systems? Describe the fanciest place you have ever installed one. Tell me about your most difficult client. And by the way, how many milli-amps of current does a SecuriCam 5000-K draw?

If you are going to stand a chance of convincing anyone that you are just installing the home-security system, you need to know the answers to all these questions and more. That's why cover for action gets deep: so deep that in a sense you are not yourself anymore, except in a tiny, sealed-away kernel of your mind. This is what undercover law enforcement officers deal with all the time.

Early on in my training, I set myself little exercises just to help me get used to lying. For example, I'd go to a random Starbucks. When they asked my name, I'd say, "Gillian." Not once did anyone question it, or look at me funny, or even pause. "Your americano will be ready over there, Gillian." I realized that I could walk around telling lies—even pretty obvious ones—all day and almost nobody would notice or care. For an aspiring clandestine officer, that's excellent news.

As my training continued, I started constructing more elaborate untruths. On planes, I would strike up conversation over the armrest. I would tell the passenger next to me I was going to a family reunion and talk their ear off about my uncle Carlos, a fictional used-car salesman from Albuquerque. Or I would say I was headed to a trade fair and bore them to tears with details of the copper wire industry—details I would make up on the spot. Remember that guy who insisted on pouring out his life story during your long-delayed flight to Sioux Falls the Wednesday before Thanksgiving? Yeah, that guy could have been a junior intelligence officer practicing lies.

The idea of all this is to probe the limits of how little people care about strangers—or even notice them. Everyone is the hero of their own story. Most others are minor characters at best. From an evolutionary point of view, this is adaptive: to avoid danger to our squishy bodies, we need to stay focused on ourselves. If our ancestors had spent too much time wondering about others, they might have fallen into a ravine or gotten bushwhacked by a leopard. A great deal of intelligence tradecraft is built on this kind of fundamental insight about evolutionary psychology.

Having learned this lesson, any undercover officer can start to build a story. Rule No. 1: Don't make your alter ego too different from yourself. Building a cover legend takes a lot of patience, practice, and psychological malleability. You don't want to make life harder for yourself by pretending to be someone who is the 180-degree opposite of you—that's too much to keep track of, not to mention too likely to trigger suspicion. Instead, you want to create a character maybe five or ten degrees off. For example, Andy Bustamante is ambiguously brown. If I decide to call myself Paddy McGuinness, say, or Tanjiro Kamado, it's going to raise questions I would rather not have to answer. So I will be Alex Hernandez instead. Like me, Alex will be a US Air Force veteran. I will have the same number of siblings, although I might switch their genders. I will have the same star sign, and so on.

Rule No. 2: Make it boring as hell. At Langley, we learn about the distinction between short- and long-term memory. In the human brain, these are governed by separate systems. Short-term memory consists of a buffer of maybe twenty seconds on average. Behind that, there's a process that decides what's important enough to copy to long-term storage. As an intelligence operative, you want to get left on the cutting-room floor.

Balthazar Y. Magnifico Jr., international blackjack professional and jetpack enthusiast, is going to attract too much attention, provoke too many questions. Again, Alex Hernandez is a prime example of this principle in action. I got the idea for his professional background from Dianna, our linguist. I don't remember the context, but Dianna once said, in passing, that the perfect story includes a boring business that is internationally recognized but totally overlooked — like a manufacturing company that makes something you'd find in any bathroom, kitchen, or office around the world. The officer could pose as a middle manager, à la Michael Scott from *The Office* — wholly unimpressive and forgettable. The genius of Dianna's story is that it virtually guaranteed no follow-up questions and nobody asking for a business card. So Alex comes from a forgettable town, works in a boring industry, and carries an unimportant job title. His sole purpose in life is work, documentation, and file organization. Any questions? No? Good. Are you half asleep already? Yes? Good.

Alex Hernandez needed a reason to make multiple visits to Falcon. I decided that the company he worked for—let's call it Acme Commercial, Inc.—was thinking of expanding its operations in Falcon's region and experimenting with securing a local supplier. As any MBA or middle manager who's listened to enough business podcasts can tell you, Acme would naturally start with small orders, to test the waters. Was there excess supply they could snap up cheaply? Was the product itself of high enough quality? After a few test shipments, the company would decide that the experiment had succeeded, and would start talking to larger manufacturers. Over a number of months and years, Acme would work its way up through bigger and bigger partnerships, placing larger and larger orders. Acme could keep expanding like this ad infinitum. Theoretically, Alex Hernandez could still be pursuing his completely fictitious quest for cheaper suppliers, even today. It's not spying. It's just good business.

Speaking of which, it's important to note that Acme Commercial, Inc., was one of millions of new businesses registered each year. It had a real website and a real email address, which I would check every so often. To anyone who chose to look into the matter, Alex would indeed appear to be the genuine article. He would have spiffy business cards and a LinkedIn profile outlining his achievements in the fast-paced world of forgettable professionals. Nobody would be any the wiser. Unless, of course, they had inside information that told them otherwise—if, say, Alex Hernandez got sloppy and let his cover slip, or if he was outed by a mole inside the Agency. If that were ever to happen, Andy Bustamante would be in severe danger.

Given that an insider was working for Falcon and against CIA, this last possibility was our biggest concern. I knew that I could hold down my cover story in the field, but until the Falcon House counterintelligence division figured out where their leaks were coming from and how to plug them, I remained unable to protect myself from exposure by an internal bad actor. But since I *did* have control over my own potential screwups, at least, I resolved to do what I could to make my cover as airtight as possible — knowing that my efforts might only take me so far.

Once I had figured out the details of my cover for action, I sat down with James for a series of roleplaying conversations to test this new story. We began with lower-stakes interactions, like meeting a chatty stranger at the grocery store. Alex would tell them his name, where he was from, what he did for a living, a little about his family, all without any weird pauses or hiccups.

The goal of this exercise is not perfect recall: it's just to seem unremarkable. For example, if somebody asks me the year I got married, I can immediately say it was 2010. But if the same person asks how long I've been married, I'd have to figure it out. Immediately blurting out, "Fifteen years, two months, five days!" would seem strangely specific... and for that reason, too memorable. Instead, I'd say something like, "Oh, now let's see. We were married in 2010, so...oh my gosh, that's how many years already? Time flies, doesn't it?"

For a similar reason, we try to dress conservatively while we're operational. If you're wearing a T-shirt with a curse word on it, or you have your hair in a purple mohawk, or your earrings are the size of softballs, that's too memorable. That one dude you once saw acting shifty and you were sure they were undercover? I can tell you with 100 percent confidence they were not. At least, they were not US trained. The real operator is the person in the background who is acting so normal you don't even notice.

In the next phase, James tested my story and knowledge about Acme Commercial, Inc. What were my volume targets for the year? Was I on track to meet them? How did we ship domestically? How about internationally? What were the pros and cons of our newest products and current accounting methods? And on and on.

After that, we moved on to higher-stakes situations: encounters with people who are trained to look for suspicious characters. For example, what if I witnessed a car accident and the police asked me for a statement? They might ask why I was in town, who I was meeting with, what line of business I was in. I'd have to keep my story straight and pass the sniff test.

While the stakes in this last phase of practice were higher, these scenarios all fell short of actual interrogation. Undercover operatives in the Intelligence Community and law enforcement undergo special training for that, and it's a good deal nastier than a simple roleplay. I would find myself falling back on that crucial training, as we will see, before our Falcon assignment was through.

While I talked up a storm in character with James in Wolf, a team of artists back at Langley got to work creating alias documents in the name of Alex Hernandez. I would need all the regular, obvious stuff, whatever documentation it would make sense for Alex to have, plus pocket litter to match. These fine details would really make Alex Hernandez come to life.

One of the most amusing things about the team of artists who work for CIA is that it's almost impossible for an artist to be granted the highest level of security clearance — not because they're untrustworthy or unpatriotic, but because almost everyone who went to art school did drugs at some point in their life. To get around this, the Agency often winds up giving them a lower level of clearance and compartmentalizing which of them does what. For example, one artist might do the text of a document while another does the photo, and so on.

As any private investigator or law enforcement officer can tell you, there are some best practices for conducting physical surveillance. In the final stage of my preparation, I ordered from Langley three copies of a wall-sized custom map of Kestrel, the Falcon capital. When you are doing undercover operations, you need to be acutely aware of your surroundings at all times. So CIA maintains a crack team of cartographers. They produce reference maps specifically in support of CIA finished intelligence. For example, the maps don't just show a park, they show every little detail, no matter how small or informal.

At the Wolf office, we displayed one copy of the map on the wall in our largest room, which happened to be Beverly and Luke's shared office. We put up the second copy in James's office, which was more secure than the others. On this copy, we used color-coded thumbtacks to mark locations—mainly places to avoid. Blue was for gathering places, like schools and houses of worship, that tend to attract a lot of people who are not trained but are vigilant; think of the anxious parents and teachers at a school, always on the lookout for any threat to the kids. Yellow was for guarded commercial sites, like banks and high-end stores; these might not attract big crowds, but they would likely have a lot of technological surveillance, like closed-circuit cameras. Red was for government sites like police stations, which would have both trained guards and camera arrays. All these hot spots—red, yellow, blue—would increase our visibility and conversely decrease the sphere within which we could control who saw us and for how long. All were best avoided.

The third copy of our map was kept under lock and key, to be brought out only when it was time to start planning operations. This copy was laminated so we could draw all over it with dry-erase markers. We would share knowledge about interesting locations. I might circle a pedestrianized street where cars couldn't tail us. I would look for restaurants and cafés to investigate for use as possible meeting spots. I would seek out locations to stash items for future use; some of the best spots were little parks that an out-of-towner might reasonably visit but that weren't teeming with potential witnesses. For example, if I had been looking at Washington, DC, I would not have picked the Lincoln Memorial, which gets millions of visitors every year. But I might have taken a second look at the memorial to Japanese internment during World War II, which is not high on most tourists' lists but sits in a tranquil (and secluded) plaza built in the style of a Zen garden. There's a reason to go there—maybe you read about it in the Lonely Planet guide and just had to check it out—but you can pretty much guarantee that it won't be crowded.

Equally important were the routes we planned to take between locations. A fundamental tool used by the Intelligence Community is what we call the surveillance detection route, or SDR. These are paths designed to give you a lot of opportunities to catch sight of anyone who might be following you. We would practice a particular type of route that would allow us to look behind us as we went or filter out innocent bystanders.

Along the way, we would do a lot of shopping, although generally not for anything glamorous, simply because the Agency would not take kindly to a reimbursement request for a $3,000 pair of shoes or whatever. The best item to shop for would be something small but unique, giving you a reason to head for the one store in a five-mile radius that might have it: let's say that coveted Michael Bolton album you've been looking for on vinyl. Ideally, it would take a bit of time to either locate a mint copy of *Soul Provider* or establish that the store didn't have it. If you were being tailed by a surveillance squad, those few minutes would give them an opportunity to rotate the officer following you, which could work to your advantage for reasons that I'll have to leave up to your imagination. We'd just need to make sure that the stopover—and the route in general—lasted long enough that anyone following us was unlikely to be doing so by coincidence. In planning this all out, of course, we'd need to estimate the length of time needed to determine that, bearing in mind the route is likely to take a lot less time in the evening than during the morning rush hour.

The challenge, of course, is to do all this without *looking* like you're doing anything in particular. To remain unremarkable, always. Like so much of what real-life undercover officers do, it's intricate, painstaking work.

We couldn't take any of our maps into the field, of course: being caught with gear like that would be way too suspicious. So I spent hours poring over these maps, committing locations and routes to memory. This was rote memorization, like a student with flash cards. When we developed enough confidence, Tasha, James, and I would test each other's knowledge. One of us would look at the map while the other would call out a proposed route through the city, remembering every turn, every road crossing. Then we would start throwing wrenches in the works. What if Ninth Street is closed that day? Then I'll take West. What if there's construction on the north side of West? And so on.

For the Cell as a whole, assigning setup and case management to me came with considerable security advantages compared to the traditional ways of doing things. I was the only point of connection between the Cell and Langley and therefore, with any luck, the only Cell member visible to any Falcon moles who might be paying attention. What's more, if Falcon intelligence were to put a tail on me, they wouldn't compromise any intelligence-gathering because I, not being a case officer, wouldn't be doing any. If they interrogated the people I spoke to, those folks would say, truthfully, that the conversation was all small talk and boring administrivia. Nothing remotely suspicious.

But of course, this did not mean there was no risk to me personally. In order to allow our case officers to stay in the shadows, the cell model relied on making me unusually visible and vulnerable. I might not have been a case officer. I might not have been talking turkey with Falcon bigwigs. But loading a dead drop for a case officer is still an act of espionage, and in many countries, including the US, the penalty for espionage is death.

My first trip inside Falcon was not about carrying out operations so much as just getting the lay of the land and creating a history of documented travel and business meetings for Alex Hernandez. Nevertheless, it would turn out to be a shit show.

It started out smoothly enough. Early on the morning of my flight out of Wolf, I went into the office and punched in a code to open the bomb-proof box that held everyone's documents. Inside, paperwork and other paraphernalia belonging to different officers were held together with a state-of-the-art solution known as...rubber bands. Occasionally, these would perish, spilling their contents into the bottom of the box, making you dig for your stuff.

Thankfully, that had not happened that day. On the desk, I made a neat stack of Andy Bustamante's documents and bound them together. I put Andy's stuff into the bomb-proof box and distributed Alex's papers and pocket litter about my person in what I hoped was a convincing manner. Then it was time for the final, decisive step. Alex Hernandez was not married (although he was perpetually engaged), meaning that unlike Andy Bustamante, he didn't wear a wedding ring.

Jihi and I own several matched pairs of wedding rings. One pair is wood, another is gold, and so on. We have a strict rule that we always wear the same ring at the same time, particularly when we have to be apart from one another. But for the purposes of the next three days, I would not be Andy Bustamante. I looked down at the ring I was wearing that day: a beautiful piece made of *mokume gane,* a Japanese style of marbled metal that Jihi had picked out because it reminded her of her childhood in the Tokyo suburbs. Right about now, Jihi would be putting hers on and getting ready to come to work. I took a deep breath, slid the ring off my finger, put it with the rest of Andy Bustamante's stuff, and slammed shut the bomb-proof box before I could change my mind. With that, Alex Hernandez was ready for his close-up.

As I stepped out of the office to hail a cab, a little voice piped up in the back of my head. *You are a criminal,* it said. *Espionage is illegal under domestic and international law. If you are caught, you could quite legitimately be sent to jail for the rest of your life. You could face the firing squad.*

But then came another voice, more enthusiastic. *My God, man,* it said. *Who gets to do this?! You are traveling the world to serve your country. This is so cool!*

For a few seconds, I listened to these twin voices, paying attention to the balance between the two. Yes, the second one was louder, for sure. So I figured I was good to go. I raised my hand for the cab and I was on my way.

In accordance with the Cell's rule, I never traveled directly from Wolf to Falcon, instead connecting through a third city in the same region. Grizzly, as we will call it, was the capital of another US-friendly country. Alex Hernandez was supposedly based there as a regional representative of Acme Commercial, Inc.

Finally, late in the afternoon, I arrived at the cold concrete block that was the main airport of Kestrel. I stood in line to show my false passport. As usual, the line crawled. My mouth felt dry from the trip. My shoulders were stiff. Fellow passengers jostled and shoved each other for position in the line. My feet hurt from standing and from being stood on. But I worked hard not to let any of that get in the way of my awareness. I needed my wits about me, because in a few minutes, I was going to lie to a Falcon officer for the first time.

The line inched forward toward the border guards' kiosks. Beyond them, I could see a wall of monitors showing closed-circuit camera footage from all over Kestrel Airport. These screens were not for the benefit of the ubiquitous security personnel. Instead, the authorities had turned them outward to face the traveling public. They were a reminder: We see you. We have eyes everywhere. You are being watched.

The border guard beckoned me forward and snatched Alex Hernandez's passport out of my hand. *Keep it simple,* I told myself. *Make it as easy as possible for him to stamp that passport.* His name was written on his security badge, but I knew better than to use it to butter him up in that very American way: "You see, Robert...may I call you Robert?" Citizens of Falcon, and especially Falcon officials, don't respond well to that kind of buddy-buddy routine. Try it at the airport and it's the quickest route to secondary screening. Likewise, attempting to use my limited command of the Falcon language would be a mistake. It would make me too memorable. The best plan was just to be the same person they saw a thousand times a day: yet another dumb American, here to make a quick buck. The usual. Boring. Forgettable.

"Name?"

"Alexander Gustavo Hernandez."

"Why are you here?"

"Business."

"Hotel?"

I said the name of a big, European-owned hotel chain.

"How long?"

"A few days."

Stamp, stamp, wave. And I was in. Textbook.

It was the evening rush hour, and the taxi stand was sheer chaos.

Locals cut in line, stealing cabs from visitors and each other. Andy Bustamante might have gotten pissed off at this and tried a bit of cutting of his own, but Alex Hernandez was not that kind of guy. Besides, a foreigner who gave as good as he got? That would be too much of a story. When I finally got into a cab, it reeked of mildew and sweat. Traditional rustic music piped from the tinny speakers as we weaved through traffic. The Falcon capital rose up along the horizon, its skyline gray.

Amid Kestrel's grim concrete, my hotel room was an oasis of tranquility. The bed was large, the sheets clean. Like the rest of the hotel, the air was perfumed with a scent like fresh linen that helped to dispel Kestrel's pervasive odor of vehicle emissions and uncollected garbage. I opened my case and found a little gift from Jihi. Not a photo, of course—we wouldn't risk handing Falcon intelligence a handy portrait of a CIA targeter—but an origami lily. Jihi had learned origami as a kid in Japan: she and her mom once made 100 paper cranes together to celebrate a Buddhist festival. Early in our relationship, I brought her a bunch of Asiatic lilies, my favorite flower. After that, she learned to make lilies, too, just for me. Whenever I traveled alone, she would fold one for each day of my trip and put them in my suitcase before I left. Inside each one, she'd write a little note. Sometimes it said something Jihi liked about me. Sometimes it would be an in-joke. Sometimes it would be something naughtier. This time, it was an affirmation: "You're so smart. You got this."

*At least somebody believes in me,* I thought.

When I came down for breakfast the following morning, I was on the lookout for my minder. I already knew what to expect. Before the Cell started operating inside Falcon, Jihi and I had visited Kestrel as regular tourists. We treated ourselves to a fancy hotel, and when we checked in we saw that the mirror didn't fog when we took a shower. This might have been a cool amenity, but more likely it was because there was a camera behind it. Down in the lobby, I caught sight of a middle-aged man who seemed especially alert to his surroundings. His potbelly strained against a nylon shirt with stains under the armpits. His teeth were stained and chipped. Most likely, he was watching foreigners to supplement his income as a day laborer or a janitor.

Amid the flow of well-heeled international travelers, the surveillant was almost comically out of place. But because your average tourist or business traveler tends not to be versed in counterintelligence or surveillance-detection, these Falcon watchers don't make much of an effort to conceal themselves. That's why I call this level of monitoring "bumbling surveillance." He wouldn't be there to hunt spies. In fact, it was almost the opposite: the Falconers were spying on us. Primarily, they were looking for specific types of information (again, you'll have to use your imagination here) that they could steal for the glory of Falcon. Bumbling surveillants represent a cheap way of identifying business travelers who might be of interest and/or easy to target. They might report on, for example, questions like: Is he wearing a Rolex or a Casio? Does she leave her laptop in the hotel room when she goes for dinner? And so on. A bumbling surveillant makes this kind of basic observation. It's up to their handlers to decide whether to act.

My second minder could have been the first one's brother: potbellied, mid-forties, dressed in a sweatsuit that had seen better days. I knew the technique to deal with this. I would take the surveillant on what I like to call a rabbit run: a route designed to (a) confirm that the person you identified really is a watcher, and (b) bore them to sleep. They'd report that Alex Hernandez is dull as shit, and after that you'd be free to make your dead drops, case your locations, set up your signals, or whatever else you need to do.

I took Sweatsuit on a shopping expedition and lost him pretty quickly. The trouble was, I got lost, too. On the map, it all looked so neat and tidy, with everything clearly labeled. Real cities are not like that. Different sections of streets turn out to have different names. One street enters a square and leaves it at a completely different angle. You get turned around.

I wound up on the wrong side of the neighborhood in an open-air market. Traders glared at me over tables of cigarette lighters, crumbling plastic toys, knockoff T-shirts, soot-stained bras and panties, dubious medicines, and flimsy mugs depicting the Falcon leadership in heroic poses. Strange, foreign dishes sizzled in large pots.

Eventually, I got back on track and made it back to the hotel. I was lying on the bed, folding and unfolding Jihi's paper lily, when the phone rang. Without really thinking, I picked it up.

"Hello?"

"Welcome to Kestrel, Mister Hernandez." The woman's voice was bubbly. Friendly. Even...cute?

"Yeah, hi."

"Congratulations. Tonight, the hotel will provide you with a complimentary massage. When would you like to schedule?"

To a normal traveler, this might have seemed like a nice gesture. To someone with counterintelligence training, it's a massive red flag. A scene played out in my head. If I accepted, the masseuse would turn out to be a young woman, one specifically selected for her appeal, the way my language instructors were when I was here as a cadet, back in the day. What happened next would be recorded on video. And then I would be theirs to manipulate.

Honey traps such as this have been used throughout the history of espionage, like Mata Hari during WWII, and with good reason. People in high-stress jobs, including many who are the targets of hostile intelligence services, need to blow off steam somehow. Sometimes they do so in ways that may be unwise: alcohol, gambling, sex. These are all vulnerabilities—sources of poor decision-making.

Before every trip, Jihi would make jokes about me falling for a honey trap. "What are you going to do when some Falcon girl with a bangin' body asks you to buy her a rum and Coke?" This was Jihi's lighthearted way of addressing a serious subject: I've always been a horny bastard. On the one hand, it was embarrassing to have to worry about self-control. On the other hand, everybody has a weakness, but not everybody knows what it is. Given that Jihi and I were both in the same line of work, we could have a frank conversation on the subject, and Jihi could remind me in her gentle way that I needed to keep myself in check—for the sake of both our mission and our marriage.

The thing was, after the day I'd had, I could have used a massage. It probably was just a nice gesture by the hotel. But no: I couldn't take the risk.

I gritted my teeth. "No thank you," I said. "I have, uh...dinner plans."

"Oh. That is a shame. Sorry, Mister Hernandez."

I hung up.


Following protocol, I returned to Wolf via Grizzly. My next trip, a few weeks later, went more smoothly. It also gave me a timely lesson in operational security. When traveling in either direction between Falcon and Grizzly, I always flew on an airline controlled by the Falcon government, knowing that Falcon intelligence had full access to the manifests. If they cared to look, they would see Alex Hernandez going back and forth every few weeks, in keeping with the fiction that he lived in Grizzly and was pursuing business opportunities in Falcon. What they wouldn't know (unless they dug into the matter further) is that I always had a connecting flight between Grizzly and Wolf—a completely separate ticket booked on a third-country carrier.

This time, my main mission was to check out a possible meeting venue. James had agreed to meet a well-heeled contact of Bridge's next time he was in Kestrel. This guy was a high roller, so we needed an appropriately flashy venue. We decided to investigate the sushi bar at a fancy hotel. I cased the joint systematically, starting on the outside. At the hotel's main entrance, the concierge came out to greet me. Most international travelers would see that as a nice gesture, but for me it was a no-go, because (this being Falcon) the local police would periodically grill the desk staff about any foreigners passing through who weren't staying at the hotel. Okay, so if James did end up using this place, he would take the side entrance: no effusive greeting that way. I went in by that door and found the quietest route to the sushi bar's host stand. I requested a table, then asked to be moved a few times until I found the one with the best view of the exits. That was where James should sit. I put on my best dopey foreigner act and, under the guise of "idiot looking for the bathroom," blundered into the kitchen to check that there was an exit there that James could dart through in case of an emergency.

The next day, after finishing up Alex Hernandez's latest round of business meetings, I headed for the hotel's gym for a stress-relieving workout. By the end of it, I was sweaty and ready for a shower. But when I opened the door to my room, I found four local guys standing inside, wrist-deep in my dresser drawers. In their knockoff Gucci tracksuits and Air Jordans, these dudes looked like a lot of people you might see around Kestrel—but slightly more polished than the bumbling surveillants I was used to seeing in the lobby. As I stepped in, they hurriedly removed their hands from the drawers they had been rifling through and stood to attention, eyes wide.

*Don't panic,* I told myself. *De-escalate the situation. Act like Alex Hernandez would act: in this case, mildly confused.*

"Oh, hello," I said. "Can I help you?"

After a pause that was just a fraction too long, one of them stepped forward and said, "So sorry to disturb you, Mister Hernandez!" With a sweeping gesture, he indicated himself and his colleagues. "The cleaning crew is just finishing."

For an excruciating second or so, the five of us just stood there, eyeing each other. Andy Bustamante might have chosen sarcasm, pointing out that they weren't wearing uniforms—or, indeed, that they hadn't brought any cleaning supplies. But that would have shown too much awareness, so thank God that for the time being I wasn't Andy Bustamante.

"Well," I said, looking around. "Thank you. It's very clean."

The four guys visibly relaxed. "You're welcome," said their leader. "We're finished. Have a good night." He gathered up his colleagues and hustled out, leaving me to think about what had just happened.

Obviously, these guys weren't a real cleaning crew, any more than their threads were real Gucci. But nor were they anything like a sophisticated counterintelligence squad. And this was a crucial fact. The A-team, the folks who hunt spies, would never have let themselves be caught by me walking into a hotel room while they turned it over. They would have had a spotter outside the gym to tell them I was coming. At the very least, they would have procured overalls and maybe a can or two of Pledge.

Bottom line: if Falcon had the slightest suspicion that Alex Gustavo Hernandez might be CIA, they would have sicced a much better team on me. Instead, they assigned more of their bumbling surveillants, fundamentally no different from the potbellied middle-aged dudes I was used to seeing around the lobby, even if these ones seemed younger and trimmer and their clothes were a little nicer. Off-duty hotel workers, most likely, paid a few extra bucks to dip into American travelers' rooms at random and see what they could find. This was scattershot surveillance, taking a punt just because they could. In my room, they would have found a big fat nothing, unless Falcon had suddenly taken a keen interest in sweaty boxer briefs, brochures, and origami flowers. To an intelligence professional, a room invasion this blatant was a reassuring sign. Falcon was not onto me at all. They had no idea who I really was — not for now, at least.

Buoyed by the realization that Falcon was clueless as to my identity, I began to straighten up my stuff, taking care to look like a businessman, not a spy. If they'd planted bugs, so be it: looking for them, let alone attempting to deactivate them, would be the most suspicious thing I could have done. As naturally as possible, I pulled out my laptop to see if they'd installed anything there. I wasn't worried about the contents: this was Alex Hernandez's computer, not Andy Bustamante's, and everything on there was absolutely consistent with my story.

The problems would arise if they had put tracking software in. First, that would indicate that they were interested not just in the contents of my hard drive but in me as an individual, which would be a worrying sign in itself. Second, if they followed the laptop's travels, they would see that I always turned it off at the airport in Grizzly and didn't turn it back on again until I returned to the same airport a few weeks later — suspicious behavior for somebody supposedly working out of Grizzly.

I found nothing sinister on the hard drive, which just reassured me that these guys had been looking for a sucker, not a spy. They wouldn't have been remotely sophisticated enough to plant a tracker. Still, I assumed they had cloned the laptop, and hoped that some poor schmo at Falcon intelligence enjoyed learning all about Alex Hernandez's sales targets for the fiscal year.

Not much later, I went in for my third visit. This time, I took my bumbling surveillant belt shopping. I visited umpteen separate stores, trying on belts made of canvas, leather, the skin of a manta ray. My minder checked out after a while, and I enjoyed the idea of him reporting that he'd spent the morning following around a belt fetishist. Then I sought out a market like the one I had blundered into before and made a beeline for the best-smelling food stall. The trader, an elderly woman, pantomimed how to eat the thing she was selling: some kind of eyeball. Or maybe a small fried lizard? Or maybe a small lizard that ate an eyeball? I closed my eyes and chomped down. It was crunchy, oily, and delicious.

# PART IX
# STORM WARNING

## SCIMITAR

For Falcon intelligence, recruiting Scimitar was a bonanza. He exposed the locations where US officers carried out clandestine operations, as well as the phone numbers they used to communicate. He handed over copies of notes from meetings. He revealed secret US facilities. Falcon now had an intelligence arsenal they could use at will or trade nefariously with other US adversaries.

After this initial leak, Scimitar did not stop cooperating with Falcon intelligence. We don't know exactly what information he gave them. But espionage has its standard operating procedures, and we can make an educated guess. Most likely, he moved on to more general debriefings, similar to the one Jihi and Dianna carried out with the Badger military commander. The Falconers would seek to understand how CIA works: what training looks like, how the organization is structured, and so on. Scimitar would get paid for each debriefing. We may never know the full extent of his betrayal. But we do know that it went on for years.

This is how it often goes with moles: they can't stop, even if they want to. The infamous traitor Aldrich Ames provides a classic example. By June 1985, just a month after he became a traitor, Ames had already given the KGB at least five pounds of classified documents and unmasked perhaps a dozen high-ranking US intelligence sources in Russia. In return, the Soviets paid him $50,000 in cash — the equivalent of around $140,000 today. At the time, Ames said he saw this as a "one-time deal." It was anything but.

"I'm still puzzled as to what took me to the next steps," Ames told Senate investigators after his capture. From the outside looking in, there is not much to puzzle over: Ames's handlers had him addicted to easy money, pure and simple. He would continue serving them for almost a decade, betraying hundreds of names and raking in almost $3 million — in today's terms, about $8.5 million. Among other luxuries, he bought himself a new house and a Jaguar sports car, paying for both in cash.

Of course, current information would fetch a much higher price than mere recollections. Here, Scimitar was at a disadvantage compared to Ames. But that still didn't leave him without options. With apologies to fans of *Men in Black,* you can't delete a person's memories — and that includes their address book. People on both sides of Langley's razor-wire fence have reasons for wanting to keep contacts warm, and most of those reasons are entirely legitimate: friendship, networking, future business opportunities. It's much the same as in any profession: schmoozing makes the world go round. Scimitar had gotten his job in high finance through a former CIA officer who now worked for the same company, and there is nothing inherently untoward about that.

Scimitar would have left the Agency with a Rolodex full of people who still worked there. Meeting up with them — inside the United States or out — would have been as easy as a phone call (likely not an email, which would leave a trail). Some may have been disgruntled. Some may have wanted out. He could have given them an outlet to vent about their colleagues or make vague promises of a job in the private sector; the Cell did both with Bridge, the third-country military engineer.

It's important to note that these people almost certainly had no idea that Scimitar was doing anything untoward. Case officers are trained to seem as innocent as possible. They don't push too hard, knowing that there are people like Jihi behind the scenes who can take scraps of information and stitch them together to create a devastating tapestry. For exactly that reason, Scimitar would have tried to keep his interactions with current CIA workers banal.

One common ploy is employment—your own or somebody else's. This would have given him a perfect excuse to pump his former colleagues for information. Maybe he spoke to Dave, a buddy from Falcon House. "I'm thinking of getting back in," Scimitar might have said. "Would that be a smart move?"

Dave probably winced at that. "They brought in this outside team. Mostly counterterrorism people. I don't understand it. The dude they put in charge is a real loose cannon."

Scimitar wouldn't have yanked that thread too hard. Instead, maybe he went next to another former colleague, Denise. "Hey, I just got a résumé from a guy who's running something for Falcon House, but it seems like he's not one of us. What do you think of him?"

"Oh, you mean Andy Bustamante?"

"Yeah…that's the one. Tell me about him."

## JIHI

A few months into our mission, the relationship I had struck up with Titan—our local partner in Wolf—was paying big dividends. Each month, Titan would share data with us. A large part of my job was combing through this information and comparing it against the other databases I had available, including the names from Bridge. I was mining for gold nuggets of data on high-value targets that I could piece together into something actionable. But simply scrubbing through millions of items would have been inefficient, not to mention mind-numbing. Instead, I ran creative searches against the data, asking myself: What if I queried it this way? What if I compared those results with these ones? And so on.

This says something about the mindset required of a targeter. Case officers are trained to identify what they want and make a beeline for it. For targeters, it's more nebulous: we need to be curious about the world in general. It's like how Andy and I treat coffee shops: Andy wants to get in, get his cup of joe, and leave, whereas I like to linger a while, see who's there, soak in the atmosphere. Who knows what interesting stuff might be happening?

When you're fully immersed in a data set, sometimes you get a familiar feeling, almost like déjà vu. You go back, run some related searches, see if anything clicks. One day, a familiar name popped out from one of my searches. Call him Alfred MacGuffin. Langley knew that MacGuffin was a senior Falcon intelligence officer. Judging by his recent travel history, it seemed he was being restationed to Wolf. That was interesting information, and for Langley and the broader US Intelligence Community, the decision to send MacGuffin to Wolf might say something about Falcon's wider strategy in the region. But for the Cell, which was focused on gaining intelligence directly from human sources, MacGuffin's presence in Wolf was not an urgent matter. A prize like that would take years to get close to. We already had one white whale: Zefram, the suspected Falcon intelligence officer under cover as a diplomat in Wolf. But Zefram, with his extreme caution and near-total lack of any pattern of life, was proving as elusive as ever. No, if we were going to try to seriously cultivate a new target, we'd need someone more attainable.

Just to be sure, I did a little extra digging. That was when I noticed something else: an anomaly. I can't say exactly what it was: the method I used is deeply classified. But suffice it to say, it was an inconsistency that suggested that somebody on the Falcon side had messed up their cover persona. Just for a moment, the mask of Falcon intelligence, typically rock-solid, had slipped.

The anomaly was enough for me to realize that there was somebody else partnered with MacGuffin: a young woman in her twenties. She wasn't his daughter or his wife, we knew that much. His girlfriend? Unlikely. MacGuffin was way too security conscious to risk an extramarital affair. All signs pointed to one conclusion: his companion was a junior officer from Falcon intelligence, one deemed promising enough to be assigned as the protégée of one of the most powerful men in the organization.

Let's call her Converse. I ran her name past Langley, too, and came back with…nothing. There was no trace of her in any of our databases. It seemed she had never so much as left Falcon before, at least in an official capacity. Nobody at CIA was tracking her, and under the finders-keepers logic of intelligence work, that meant the Cell had first dibs. A young woman on her first overseas assignment, being mentored by a top-ranked Falcon intelligence officer? Yes, that was a target profile I could work with. I decided I would find a way to get to her if it killed me.

Converse could be the start of something big. If we played our cards right, we might get the chance to make her into a mole of our very own inside Falcon intelligence. At that point, we would potentially have eyes not just on Falcon's intelligence priorities in its own region but on the sources it was running against us within the United States. If we got really lucky, we might just catch this Falcon mole who had been plaguing CIA. "The Keys to the Kingdom"—at CIA, that was what we called an opportunity to turn a foreign agent into a US intelligence source.

I began compiling a dossier on Converse. In contrast to Zefram, who was a generation older, this time it was relatively easy. Converse had a public social-media profile—all under her cover persona, of course. This didn't surprise me. Initially, intelligence agencies around the world (including CIA) forbade their people from creating profiles. But by this time, social media had become so ubiquitous that it would be more suspicious *not* to have a presence online, so the agencies did an about-face and started encouraging their people to be on social media. (Although, ironically enough, I shy away from social media myself.)

In the years leading up to our deployment, Falcon had grown particularly confident letting its citizens use the internet. And if nothing else, social media was proving a cost-effective way to root out domestic dissidents, always a bigger concern for a dictatorship than any penetration by foreign intelligence. But the Falcon government's toleration of social media also made a smorgasbord of data available to CIA targeters like me, open source and ready to use. Thanks, Falcon.

From Converse's presence on social media, a clear picture emerged. You could tell from the photos she posted that, like most people her age, she had a lot of friends and she enjoyed hanging out with them regularly. She was having fun—albeit squeaky-clean, girly-girl fun: shopping and food. There were no pictures of her sloppy in a bar at 1 a.m. In fact, there were few pictures that could even be placed geographically. Her profile was just detailed enough that it wouldn't look weird. If anything, it was a little *too* normal—a classic intelligence officer social media page, in other words.

I put myself in Converse's shoes. New in town, on her first overseas posting, she would no doubt be feeling lonely. She would be on the lookout for new, local friends and things to do with them. She would be under pressure to impress her mentor by doing what case officers do: building contacts. I figured we could use all of that.

In another time and place, I might have matched Converse with the case officer who was closest to her in age, twenty-something Tasha. Instead, I thought this was the perfect opportunity to bring in our other fierce female: the feisty, forty-something Beverly. Like Converse, Beverly was bubbly and sociable. She had built a successful career in a man's world, a challenge that Converse was facing now. Best of all, the match would take advantage of a cultural quirk.

Beverly was raring to go, provided we could insulate her against the special risks involved in going after a fellow intelligence officer. With her training, Converse was much more likely than your average source (engineer Bridge, say, or businessman Kingpin) to realize that Beverly was collecting on her. Falcon intelligence might then try to flip Beverly's loyalty, through blackmail or otherwise. They might put surveillance on her, just as we had spied on Zefram. That could lead them to Luke, which could lead them to the contacts he'd been working. We weren't worried that Luke or Beverly would be arrested or harmed in Wolf—targeting them in a US-allied country would have been too audacious, even for Falcon intelligence. But if they went into Falcon, as we expected them to do in due course, they would be in danger. On a more mundane level, if Luke and Beverly got blown, the Falconers would have no hesitation in selling their identities to other US adversaries, permanently locking them out of the juiciest case work and effectively tanking their careers.

Reporting on this case would go only to a subset of Falcon House: the counterintelligence division, run by the heron-looking guy with the icy stare who had briefed us on the situation with the mole. In fact, it would be so compartmentalized that only a few people at Langley would know that we were targeting Converse—or even that she existed.

Inside the Cell, however, everyone would know about it. That was by design: part of the new way of doing things was to bring in multiple perspectives on each case. We would review the case more frequently. Will would use his methods to detect any monitoring on Beverly's communication platforms. Luke would be on guard. Like any operating undercover officer, Beverly would travel to and from meetings with Converse via surveillance detection routes—SDRs—the way Andy was doing when he traveled inside Falcon.

Was this enough to mitigate the risks? We convened a discussion with Beverly and laid out our wildest fears and hopes. The conclusion that we reached with her: intelligence is a high-stakes game, but a game nonetheless. We never met an intel officer who didn't see it that way. And in any game, you sometimes have to risk it all.

Next, we needed to find a hook for the relationship we wanted Beverly to start with Converse—a point of mutual interest between the two of them. Work stuff wouldn't do in this scenario: it would be alerting to take too much interest in Converse's job early on. Besides, undercover officers hate being asked about their work, simply because it is exhausting to have to remember all the details of a cover story all the time. So if we really wanted Converse to vibe with Beverly, it had to be over something extracurricular.

The available information was enough for me to put together a list of Converse's likely extracurricular activities: brands she favored, food and drink she liked, a handful of sports she might play. I gave Beverly the list and asked her if she was into any of the stuff on there.

Beverly didn't even look at it. "If I'm not," she said, "I'm sure I *could* be."

I was starting to realize that the word "no" was not in Beverly's vocabulary. If she thought it would help her advance a juicy case, she would have discovered a sudden love for parkour or pigeon racing or cutthroat pinochle. Talk about taking one for the team.

Beverly sipped champagne and surveyed the party. It was Bastille Day at a French expat's house in Wolf, not the worst place to be sent on the government's dime. Right on schedule, Converse glided into the room in a little black cocktail dress, accompanied by Alfred MacGuffin, her senior mentor.

Beverly couldn't bump Converse with MacGuffin right there: the risk was too great that a seasoned veteran like him would smell a rat. If all else failed, Beverly told herself, she could always follow Converse into the ladies' room and do the bump there.

"Finally, some peace and quiet," she would say. Or, "Nice watch." Or whatever. Beverly was confident, as Beverly usually was. Something would turn up. It always did.

Beverly kept her eye on Converse as MacGuffin shepherded her around the room, introducing her to various clumps of people. She noted that Converse behaved as a quiet observer, smiling and nodding rather than putting herself at the center of attention. She was graceful, demure. A perfect target for hard-charging Beverly.

After a while, MacGuffin made an excuse and peeled off to talk to other men of his own level, leaving Converse alone. Beverly saw her opening.

"Typical men, huh?" said Beverly, sidling up to Converse. "Leaving us ladies to do the real work. See over there?" She pointed to Luke, who was busy schmoozing. "My husband's doing the same thing."

"Oh, which one is your husband?"

Beverly gestured with her champagne flute. "See the younger guy there, in the suit? That's him."

Converse looked at Beverly in awe. Women in Falcon were typically expected to marry older men, sometimes significantly older. Running into one who had reversed that age gap must have been like seeing a unicorn at Walmart. And with that, the hook was in. But Beverly still needed a plausible reason for them to meet again. To find it, she would have to do some fishing.

"So, what brings you to Wolf?" Beverly asked, knowing from my targeting package what the phony answer would be.

Converse said she worked at the Falcon equivalent of the Bureau of Paperwork.

"No kidding." Beverly smiled. "But let's not talk about work. Do you miss Falcon?"

They riffed for a couple of minutes on all the things they missed from home: food, friends, family. Then Converse said, "Plus, I can't find a good place to play tennis here."

Of all the potential extracurriculars on my list, this was the one we most hoped for. Tennis, a two-person sport played on courts that are often tucked away behind buildings or high fences, represents a perfect opportunity to speak openly with less fear that anyone might spot you. Best of all, Beverly didn't even need to fake an interest in the game: she had been an avid tennis player since she was a little girl. In the past, she had even played competitively. One of the first things she had done when she was posted to Wolf was find a good tennis club in the city.

"I love tennis!" Beverly gushed, genuinely excited. "Want to come play at my club?"

"Are you serious? I would love to!"

## ANDY

Beverly still had other cases going on for other parts of the Agency, but for now, she put everything besides Converse on the back burner. Every other member of the Cell rallied around her to offer support. James and Dianna helped her understand cultural nuances she might be able to exploit, as she had done with the "big sister" relationship. Tasha swapped notes on dealing with Falconers unused to strong women. We all participated in brainstorming sessions.

In the beginning, we dissected everything. Converse arrived six minutes late. What did that mean? Was it because she had to brief a surveillance team? She sent Beverly a text right after they met. Was that a way of tracking her? Was she probing to see if Beverly was running an SDR? She asked Luke's zodiac sign. Was that because she thought Luke might be a fake husband? We would pick all these questions apart in our conversations in the bullpen.

Over time, a pattern emerged, and it gave us confidence. Converse always ran late because, as a diligent person, she couldn't say no to last-minute taskings from the boss (Jihi had the same problem). She texted so often because she liked Beverly and was generally a nice person. As for the zodiac stuff, it seemed she was just kind of...into astrology, which fit her girly personality. Will's work confirmed that unless the Falconers were using some technology we couldn't even imagine, all Beverly's devices seemed clean. Her apartment wasn't bugged. Neither she nor Luke reported suspicious activity.

Aside from this, Beverly and Converse really clicked (it would have been hard not to click with Beverly). In addition to tennis games, the two of them were making joint outings to the spa and getting together to check out little out-of-the-way coffee spots. Whatever the female equivalent of a bromance is, this was it.

If Converse was making a play for Beverly, she was doing kind of a sucky job at it. Playing tennis together had been Beverly's idea. More significantly, they had gone to Beverly's club. As the relationship evolved, Converse continued to allow Beverly to choose meeting times and locations—the spa, the cafés, and so on. If she was trying to develop Beverly into a source, she was making the same error that I had made way back in training: surrendering control to the target, the way I did with Major Bondoy.

Besides, Converse seemed genuinely to look up to Beverly, and we knew that there were important, deep-seated cultural reasons why this should be the case. Girls in Falcon are taught to be submissive: taking control of a relationship is not something they learn to do. But Beverly was a natural at it. Converse had never met anyone quite like her. "Teach me your secrets," she seemed to say. How do you stick up for yourself at work? How are you an equal partner in your marriage? For a Falcon woman, these were tantalizing mysteries. We may have been on the back foot following the mole's destructive betrayals, but America's open, more egalitarian society did give us certain significant cultural advantages over our rivals.

## JIHI

While Beverly worked her magic on Converse, we continued to chip away at Zefram, our white whale. We were coming up against an iron law of intelligence: on its own, the technology is just not that useful, even if it's state-of-the-art and delivers you a wealth of information about your subject. Out of context, it turns out, most conversations sound like gibberish.

We overheard a bunch of exchanges between Zefram and his mom, for example, from which we learned that Cousin Whatsit had done well in her exams, that Uncle So-and-So was getting a promotion, and that after all these years Mrs. Thingamabob had finally divulged her recipe for stew. We picked up back-and-forth between the Zeframs and the super at their apartment complex about getting stuff repaired or hanging pictures on the wall.

We also heard a lot about the Zeframs' personal life — especially when it came to their son, Zefram Jr. It seemed that the Zeframs were helicopter parents. They worried constantly about Zefram Jr. Was he all right? How was he feeling? If we took him to the park this weekend, would that be okay?

Andy and I didn't have kids yet, but I knew enough to know that this was not the way most people spoke about their children. Usually what you heard would be bragging — "Little Johnny got an A+ in art class!" — or complaining — "Little Johnny called me a bitch the other day, what a brat!" Not the Zeframs. With them, the overriding sense was one of concern. Then again, Zefram Jr. was an only child, so perhaps that made sense.

In any event, it was all useless to us. The one thing we never picked up was any talk about work. Occasionally, Zefram would call to arrange a driver, but that was about it. In keeping with his MO, he was very cautious. Meanwhile, Dianna was driving herself bonkers translating endless chatter about groceries and doctors' appointments. To make sense of any of this, we would need to know what to focus on. And to know what to focus on, we'd have to pair our data with other information about the target. Lucky for us, other information was on the way.


While his wife wowed Converse, Luke was busy doing some schmoozing of his own. At a second-tier party in Wolf, Luke ran into Wander, a

Falcon fixer based in the city. Wander prided himself on being able to cater to every whim of his well-heeled clients, from bookings at the finest restaurants to bags of the freshest cocaine. In the past, Luke might have dismissed Wander as a useless figure: no government in its right mind would hand out a security clearance to a guy like that. But now, Luke saw things differently: armed with targeter logic about seeing sources as nodes in a network, Wander suddenly seemed very interesting.

Wander worked with, or at least knew about, every high-ranking Falcon official and businessperson passing through Wolf. Better yet, he loved to gossip.

"So there's this one guy," Wander would say. "He comes through here maybe once a month, he's high up in the leadership. A real freak show, oh my God. And he's really into African girls. So every time he's in town, I have to find African girls who are willing to . . . Well. It's a pain in the ass, anyhow."

"Mm-hmm." Luke nodded, smiled, and sipped his scotch, silently banking the information. Who knew when a nugget like that might come in handy?

Using my knowledge of the social scene in Wolf, I made sure that Luke kept just-so-happening to show up at the same parties as Wander. Luke kept Wander interested with the vague implication that, somewhere down the line, he might be able to send some visiting US dignitaries his way. These would represent a step up in Wander's career. Unfortunately for Wander, Luke could never actually deliver on that hazy promise: it would be a security risk, and besides, there was no way Luke was going to imperil his reputation by sending powerful Americans to a lowlife like Wander. But he kept stringing Wander along by giving him a heads-up when trade delegations of other nationalities were about to pass through town.

Luke's style was very different from those of our other case officers. James would sweep contacts along with irresistible energy. Tasha's opening gambit was self-deprecating humor. Beverly would ask them endless questions about themselves. Luke, on the other hand, was the master of silence and patience — two characteristics typically not shared by the kind of hard-charging person who hires a fixer like Wander. Luke would smile and nod until you felt compelled to say something. It was all done with such charm that you'd never know he was just giving you enough rope.

All this together encouraged Wander, according to his mood, to brag about his clients or dump all over them. Either way, it was useful stuff. Wander generally kept names out of it — his business required a certain amount of discretion, after all — but for a trained targeter, the information he did provide was enough. I would take it and cross-reference it with travel data, phone records, and some other stuff too secret to talk about. In this way, I would begin to piece together who was who. I began building up yet another spider diagram, this time with Wander at the center. This one overlapped with the data from another source and even to some extent with the spider diagram from Bridge, meaning that we now had information on the same contacts derived from several sources: a holy grail of targeting if ever there was one.

There was one particular client about whom Wander liked to brag and complain equally, a well-connected fellow Falconer, based in Wolf. He did something with the Falcon embassy. The more Wander talked, the more convinced I became that his client was Zefram.

For Wander, three things stood out about our white whale.

One: Zefram was boring in the extreme. We've already said that Wolf was well known as a party town: that was one of the things that attracted me to the assignment. But while Wander's other clients might snort cocaine off a prostitute's thigh, Zefram did nothing like that. In fact, he usually seemed dour, a stick-in-the-mud. Grumpy, even. To Wander, this was a source of irritation. Zefram only hired Wander for little piecemeal jobs like finding drivers (although Wander knew Zefram was also getting drivers from other sources). These jobs were fine, but what Wander really wanted was a bigger payday: A party. A big dinner. An orgy. Zefram didn't do any of that stuff.

Two: there was a particular bathhouse in the city that Zefram especially liked to attend (as it happened, it was the same one we had seen him visit when we surveilled his vehicles, so this was another point of confirmation). Luke realized right away how good a bump spot that could be. The bathhouse was accessible to the public (at least to male members of the public), but it would also be chock full of little self-contained rooms. Behind clouds of steam, Luke could induce Zefram to surrender his secrets — if we could find the right leverage.

Three: Zefram wanted drugs, but not the kind Wander was used to supplying. Zefram would commission the fixer to source powerful painkillers that were hard to get without a prescription. Stuff like propofol, the anesthetic "milk" that killed Michael Jackson in LA a couple of years before the Cell got going.

We naturally assumed that Zefram was using the painkillers on himself. In a business as stressful as intelligence, it wasn't unusual. This information might offer us a little leverage: if Zefram's wife didn't know, for example, there could be an implied threat of exposure, but that alone wouldn't be strong enough to make a hardened Falcon operator like Zefram play ball with CIA. The poor guy probably just had insomnia or a bad back. His nearest and dearest most likely knew and sympathized. Besides, unlike many of America's rivals, blackmail is not really CIA's strong suit.

The main problem, though, was that Zefram's need for analgesics didn't point to any unfulfilled desire: through Wander, he already enjoyed a ready supply. There was no need going unmet.

We still didn't have enough to make a bump. But the little detail about painkillers gave me an idea.

Over a new batch of butter cake (not as risky as propofol, but with a lot more sugar), I briefed Dianna on the latest revelations. I asked her to be on alert for anything medical. "Maybe he's got a condition we can help him with, something like that?"

Dianna thought for a bit. "Actually, that rings a bell." She leafed through her notes on the latest batch of information. "Yeah. Right here, Mrs. Zefram says...Oh, it's not about Zefram though. It's their son. She was making some kind of doctor's appointment for him."

When I heard that, my targeter sense started to tingle, because I knew how powerful a family member in distress could be. But I tried to contain my excitement for the time being: maybe the boy just had a sniffle. The Zeframs did seem to be overly attentive parents: blowing stuff out of proportion might just be their style.

I asked Dianna to give me the names of the doctors Mrs. Zefram had been speaking to. Wolf was a big city, but there were only so many specialists. By cross-referencing those names, we figured out with a high degree of probability what was wrong with Zefram Jr., and it was a lot more serious than a touch of the flu. The poor kid likely had cancer of the optic nerve, a form of brain tumor that typically affects young children.

It all fit. The painkillers were for the boy, not his father. Zefram Sr. was dour and grumpy all the time because he was exhausted, and we could see why: having a child with brain cancer would put a damper on anyone's party spirit.

James did a bit of background reading on potential treatments. It turned out that doctors in Falcon could operate to remove the tumor, but they might well blind the boy in the process. At leading hospitals in the United States or Western Europe, however, there would be much less risk of damage to his eyesight. We could get Zefram Jr. an appointment at one of those specialist clinics in the West. Maybe not in the United States — Zefram would still be on his guard about that — but in a friendly European country, perhaps. That done, we would save a child's sight *and*, with a little luck, unlock a treasure trove of intelligence for the United States. Compared to extortion, this was much more in CIA's wheelhouse.

As excited as we were to get started, we would still have to be careful about making the bump. It couldn't come out of the blue, not for someone as counterintelligence-savvy as Zefram. We would need a natural-seeming approach. So: priority one was for Luke to start attending that bathhouse Wander mentioned. Zefram didn't do anything according to a regular schedule, so Luke would have to go a *lot*. If they had a loyalty card, it would be worth Luke's while to get one. We all enjoyed the image of him serving America by looking at a bunch of saggy old-man butts.

Gradually — over weeks, months even — Luke would build up a pattern of attendance that would overlap with Zefram's own. He would look for openings to get talking to Zefram about anything and everything: the weather, the traffic, the temperature in the sauna. After building rapport, Luke would start steering the conversation, gently, toward kids or health or both. With a grave look on his face, Zefram would mention his son's condition. Only then would Luke be ready to come in with the generous offer of scouring his network for a doctor in the West who could help Zefram Jr.

It was going to be a long voyage to harpoon our white whale, but at last we were underway.

## ANDY

As we approached the tail end of the year, things seemed to be going great for the Cell. We were running with the terrorist-cell model, based on lessons learned from al-Qaeda, and it was fun to be on the other side of it for once. Our targeting, tech, and linguistics teammates were all working hand-in-glove with the case officers, and early indications were that the model would produce the goods. Jihi had taken information from Bridge and Kingpin and used it to chart their contacts inside Falcon, which James and Tasha were now developing as potential sources. Luke had discovered a passion for Zefram's favorite bathhouse. Beverly was working on her backhand with Converse, and had seen no sign yet of any suspicion or surveillance as a result.

We seemed to be going from strength to strength. At the same time, I kept reminding myself that it would take just one mistake for everything to go sideways. And if and when it did, I'd be the one to pay.

Six out of the seven members of the Cell were hidden from the mole in Falcon House—that was how the terrorist-cell model operated. There was one exception, the one person who did report up the chain: the case manager. Me. I was the point of contact with Langley. Sooner or later, the mole might very well catch up to me, the way CIA had caught up to bin Laden's courier. And on that day, Falcon wouldn't send four guys on a phony cleaning detail. Instead, they might send four paramilitaries in a black panel van: two to hold me down, one to cuff me, one to put the bag over my head, all four to drag me away. After that, it would be a straight line to prison, the starvation diet, the forced confession. And then, oblivion.

Both Jihi and I feared that day would come soon. Having spent years hunting down the one person a terrorist cell showed to the world, we knew how short that person's life expectancy could be.

"Look at this shit," James said. He was pointing to a local newspaper on his desk.

FERRARI UNVEILS NEW 458 ITALIA SPIDER, read the headline. Under the article was a block of classified ads. Among them, an ad stating, "4-stroke engine apprentice needed—small jobs, big paychecks."

"Ah, crap," I said. "What does the big bastard want now?"

"I guess I'm about to find out, brother. I'm seeing him next week."

For years, terrorists had been using public, freely available media— radio, newspapers, social media—to hide signals in the noise. Now we, the members of the Cell, were doing the same. I knew that "4-stroke engine apprentice" was none other than Bridge, James's military engineer contact. The ad would have meant nothing to the billions of readers who had access to it—including any car enthusiasts among Falcon intelligence. But to the Cell, it was a duress signal, like the one we received back in the spring, when James went in to meet Evade. It meant *I'm in trouble. I need an emergency meeting.*

James went to meet Bridge in what had become his natural habitat: a casino resort. Bridge met James at the bar, pairing his usual tailored suit with a look of fury.

"They put a minder on me, James. A minder! On *me*! Can you believe that?"

"Oh my God, man. I'm sorry."

"I feel like I'm under a goddamn magnifying glass!"

Bridge was used to the red-carpet, white-glove treatment. After all, his services as a talented military engineer were crucial to Falcon's silent-sub program. But lately things had begun to go south. He was asked questions at the border, where previously he was allowed to sail through. His limo showed up late to pick him up from Kestrel Airport. The concierge at the hotel was slow and disorganized. They put the wrong premium cognac in his room. Finally, they imposed on Bridge the kind of bumbling surveillance usually reserved for normies — certainly not VIPs — and this new minder was really putting a crimp in his style, particularly at the complimentary brothel.

"I'm going to quit, James. I really mean it this time. I can't take these idiots screwing things up for me anymore."

If Bridge quit, that would be devastating for us. We would lose a key node in our network. But James knew he wouldn't really do it. He liked the Falcon money too much — not to mention all the people forced to kiss his ass. Unless we told him his life was at stake, Bridge would keep riding that gravy train.

However, his many complaints did raise questions: Was this just Bridge being a spoiled brat, as usual? Had he only just noticed a minder who had been there all along? Or was there something more sinister going on?

James sipped his drink and thought. The minor inconveniences and screwups Bridge described could just be Bridge overreacting...

Or...

They could be symptoms not of low-rent surveillance, but of *increased* surveillance.

Let's imagine that the Falconers now had two separate teams taking care of Bridge: his usual protocol team, whose job it was to kiss his ass, plus a second, more sophisticated surveillance team, whose job it was to keep tabs on him, maybe gently intimidate him. They vie with each other to call the shots. The protocol team assigns him a Lincoln Continental from the airport, but at the last minute, the surveillance squad swaps it out for a Chevy Suburban they have wired, and detains the driver for a security briefing. The protocol team has booked the hotel's presidential suite for Bridge, but at the last minute the surveillance team insists that the hotel move him to room 237, where they can monitor him. Now the hotel staff have to scramble to get the Napoleon brandy to 237. Amid the confusion, the mistakes would keep piling up.

Nobody in either the protocol team or the surveillance team would seek clarification, because that would be to admit that they didn't know what they were doing, which in Falcon could have dire consequences. The result would be a concatenation of screwups very much like the one Bridge was experiencing. Was that the explanation? And if so, why was Bridge suddenly being given this treatment?

## JIHI

Luke gave me, Andy, and James an update on Wander.

"He's over the moon," Luke said. "The guy has been picking up clients left and right." Wander was enjoying multiple new referrals just that week, Luke said. All of the new clients were Falcon. Some had previously been working with fixers of other nationalities, but now they were all coming to Wander.

"Knowing him," Luke went on, "it's probably just a ploy to seem like he's more in demand."

Such a ploy would be in character for Wander, who would have no qualms about blowing smoke up Luke's ass if he thought it would impress him. Ordinarily, we might have dismissed Wander's bragging as exactly that. But this uptick in business for the Falcon fixer was coming at the same time as minders and mistakes were suddenly materializing around our non-Falcon engineer. That couldn't just be a coincidence, could it?

Meanwhile, reports were coming in from all over the world that

Falcon sources of all kinds were starting to clam up. We heard about it from case officers passing through Wolf. Then it started popping up in official communications. It didn't take long for the rot to reach our own cases.

First, Tasha noticed that it was becoming harder to meet up with Kingpin. Just when she thought she was getting somewhere with him, he began canceling their family get-togethers on short notice, with little explanation. Tasha tried to make plans through Mrs. Kingpin instead, only to be fobbed off with a variety of excuses: work, travel, and so on.

"I'm so sorry," Mrs. Kingpin told Tasha on the phone, adding, after a pause, "I know Kingpin Jr. misses playing with little Monty."

Even Converse, the bubbly young intelligence officer who respected Beverly so much, was getting more reluctant. "Work is busy," she would say. "And you know, there is a lot of tension between our countries."

In the circumstances, the latter was a weird excuse to use. Granted, there was always a degree of tension between America and Falcon. But at that time, those strains were at historic lows—on the surface, at least.

Beverly pushed back—giving people space is not really her style. When she and Converse ran into each other at another function, Beverly said, "Long time no see. You still owe me a rematch."

"I'm...sorry," Converse said to the floorboards. Where previously she was bubbly and effusive, now she visibly contorted with embarrassment. We also noticed around this time that she stopped posting to her Facebook profile. This sudden about-face in Converse's whole manner was the biggest clue yet that something was up.

Following each setback, I would meet with Andy and James to discuss it. One example of weird behavior from a single target wouldn't have amounted to much, but after a few weeks of seeing multiple sources act strangely, the warning signs were really starting to pile up.

The strange thing was that none of our people were reporting any additional surveillance. Beverly and Luke, both chasing intelligence officers, had not seen anyone following them. Will confirmed that they were not being tracked with technology, either. By this time, James and Tasha had begun traveling into Falcon to cultivate the higher-level contacts they were getting from Bridge and Kingpin. But even there, they were experiencing nothing out of the ordinary: just the same bumbling surveillance as ever. What did this all point to? We braced for... something. But what? We were about to find out.

# PART X

# HAZY WITH A CHANCE OF DEATH

## ANDY

Jihi wanted to go over the communication plan again.

"We already know the commo plan," I mumbled through a mouthful of Honey Nut Cheerios.

"Let's go over it again anyway. Primary?"

"Okay, okay. Primary, I will call you from my cell phone."

"How often?"

"Every twenty-four hours."

"At least."

"Sure, at least."

Later that morning, I was due to fly to Kestrel once again. At this point, I had been doing this kind of thing for months. I knew Kestrel like the back of my hand. I could have picked out my bumbling surveillants in a *Where's Waldo?* cartoon. This was the kind of thing I had gotten into intelligence to do. This time, I was even more excited to go in. We're seeing signs that something was in flux, but we didn't know exactly what. The Cell could be the first to figure it out, and I was, at long last, the tip of the spear.

"Okay," Jihi went on. "Secondary?"

"If I can't call from my own phone, I'll call from a...different phone."

We were doing our best to use innocuous (in the trade we call it "non-alerting") terminology in case our apartment was bugged. But "a different phone" really meant that if I thought Falcon intelligence might be closing in on me and using my cell phone signal to hunt me down, I would dump my phone, steal someone else's, and use that to alert Jihi and the Cell that I was in trouble. This commo plan of ours was not official policy: it was an additional layer of reassurance we had cooked up between ourselves.

"Good. Tertiary?"

"I'll use the email."

Meaning that if I had to go into hiding inside Falcon, I would draft an email. I would not send it, because they might track that. I would leave it in the drafts folder of an anonymous account to which only Jihi and I had access. But I'd use this method only if capture was imminent, and that seemed extremely unlikely.

A few hours later, I was standing in line at Falcon passport control, tapping my feet with impatience. The border guard at the front of the line looked about fourteen years old and was having a confused and increasingly irritable conversation with a tall African dude in a kufi hat, his long robe trimmed in multicolored brocade.

"What hotel are you staying at?" asked the guard.

"No hotel. I say I stay with family. Family!"

"What family?"

"My sister."

"Where?"

The African guy mentioned a poor district of Kestrel.

"Okay, okay. What is your sister's name?"

"Kuzivakwashe Hazvinei."

"What?! What?!"

I smiled inwardly. That was a textbook example of what you don't want to happen: confusing the guard with a convoluted story makes you memorable.

Exasperated, the security guard sent the African guy to secondary screening, with a curse. He beckoned me forward.

"Name?"

"Alex Hernandez."

"Why have you come to Falcon?"

"Business."

"Hotel?"

I said the name.

"How long are you staying?"

"A few days."

Stamp, stamp. I had gotten good at this. The teenage-looking guard handed me back Alex Hernandez's passport and waved the next person forward.

Through the windows of the taxi, the familiar sights of Kestrel materialized. Piles of snow now lined the highway shoulders, turning black from the constant pall of car exhaust. People hurried along the icy sidewalks, hunched over against the cold. As I had done before, I used the journey to acclimatize myself to the sights, sounds, and smells of Falcon.

I arrived at my lodging around dinnertime. This time, the hotel was massive, part of a complex with an open-air shopping center in the middle. An island of hospitality.

Exiting the cab, I scanned for my minder. There was nobody outside, which wasn't surprising, given how cold the weather had gotten. Crossing the immense lobby on my way to check in, I noted a guy staring into space, another inspecting the coffee machine, and a half dozen other possible suspects. I committed their faces to memory, reading their features left to right, like a book. I assigned each one a cartoonish name: Big Nose, Uncle John, KFC, Cheekbones, and so on.

In my room, I opened up the latest origami lily from Jihi. This time, the message inside was a sexy one. "Do a good job and your reward awaits in the bedroom." I allowed myself to imagine what the reward might be, and with that little hit of dopamine, I headed down to one of the hotel's bars to grab a bite and ID my tail. By now, I knew exactly what to expect. Most of the faces I memorized would be gone, leaving just one or two. One of them would follow me to the bar and position themselves where they could keep watch. Not subtle, but this was bumbling surveillance. You wouldn't expect anything else.

Crossing the lobby from the elevators to the bar entrance, I saw none of the dozen faces I spotted before. Perhaps there was one I missed? I lingered in the lobby, pretending to look at posters advertising various tourist traps. Still nothing.

I parked myself at a corner table with a good view of the whole space and ordered the dish I judged least likely to give me *E. coli*. It was dinnertime and the bar was close to full, but every other patron seemed to be engrossed in a conversation or a magazine or a smartphone. Nobody was visibly watching me. I scanned again, and again came up empty. This was strange. I told myself not to worry. Surely someone would appear to pick up my trail before I left the hotel tomorrow morning.

Getting ready for bed, I checked the weather forecast. It was good news: a breeze was supposed to blow in overnight, bringing with it clear skies and fresh air. Good: I wouldn't have to worry as much about the stinging in my eyes or the burnt-rubber taste in my mouth. I mentally ran through my plan for the next day. As usual, I would not be doing overt espionage. I would have two meetings with local suppliers and manufacturers. Between those, I would visit a little café in a quiet neighborhood to scout it as a potential meeting location. Somewhere along the way, my minder would get bored of all this and check out.

On day three, with my surveillance lulled to sleep, I would just happen to find myself in a nearby public park, where—carefully picking my moment so the tail wouldn't see me—I would stash a small device that James needed for his next operation. I visualized the place I had chosen: obscure but not suspicious for me to access. In my mind's eye, I saw my route through the city, carefully plotted on the map back in Wolf and committed to memory.

My every step was planned. All that remained was to do it. Nothing is exactly routine when you are in the field on a mission, as any paramilitary officer could tell you; but I felt like this was as close as it would get to a normal day at the office.

I woke early for my meetings. I took a shower and donned the mahogany suit I selected for the trip because it was warmer and less likely to show the inevitable soot stains. On top of it, I put on a navy-blue overcoat made of dense, heavy wool. Besides that, I was wearing long underwear, insulated gloves, and a woolen sock hat. From my time babysitting ICBMs at Malmstrom, I knew how to deal with cold. But in this environment, hostile for reasons well beyond weather, my heavy clothes carried an additional benefit: they made me feel protected, as if I were wearing armor. It was an illusion, of course, but a comforting one.

My work bag was a leather backpack. CIA training encourages you to carry a bag with two straps. If you have to run, you can strap it to your body and not worry about it flailing around. Of course, you hope never to have to test that.

Down in the lobby at 7:30 a.m., people milled about bleary-eyed, psyching themselves up to go outdoors, into the cold. I finally spotted my surveillant: a guy just hanging out, blatantly watching the elevator bank. Unlike most of the early-morning zombies, he was super-alert, as if his head were on a gimbal. He was younger than the average bumbling surveillant, maybe in his late twenties, and seemed to take more pride in his appearance, with a nice button-down shirt and slacks. He looked like a nerdy teacher's pet. In a split second, my brain assigned him a nickname: Smarty Pants.

He, like the bumbling "cleaning crew" I encountered on an earlier visit, was reassuring. But now, as I made my way from the elevator into the lobby proper, Smarty Pants approached me. In fact, now he was... waving at me? What the hell was going on?

"The Johnsons, right?" he said.

He was looking past me. I turned to see a couple of American tourists exiting an elevator. He wasn't a minder, then, just their tour guide. Out they went into the cold morning, chatting about all the sights they would see in the day ahead. But if Smarty Pants was their guy, where the hell was mine?

Through the hotel's tall glass front doors, I saw the black sedan that was waiting to take me to my meeting in a half hour. I didn't want to keep the driver waiting—that, too, might make me memorable—but at the same time, I didn't want to leave until I had identified this damn surveillant. So I started a sort of slow dance toward the exit, hamming up the bleary-eyed morning act, making my way from the elevator bank to the bagel station to the coffeepot, trying to see if somebody—anybody—was going to follow me.

Nothing.

A thought dawned in my mind. I had often spoken with James about our shared dream: that one day we would blend in so effectively, make ourselves so forgettable, that Falcon intelligence would stop bothering to follow us altogether. And if there was nobody watching me yesterday evening, and nobody watching me this morning, then that must mean . . .

"You've done it, man," said a voice in my head. "You've *done* it! You're a genius!"

In the space of a few months, I had gone from getting lost in the backstreets of Kestrel to eating grilled eyeballs to being ignored completely. I felt like Neo in *The Matrix,* when he finally perceives the ones and zeroes, green on black, that truly make up the world. *Just wait until James hears about this,* I thought. I imagined his and Tasha's faces as I gloated.

With a bagel in one hand and a cup of coffee in the other, I strode out of the front door toward my waiting chariot. Some of the hotel's warm, perfumed air exited with me, but it soon dissipated, leaving me with the harsh reality of Kestrel: the biting cold, the smell of tire tread and exhaust.

*Whenever you think you have mastered something,* said another voice in my head, *that's when you are at your most vulnerable.*

My mind flashed back to that day on the Farm when it all fell apart. I remembered my interrogator screaming in my face, his spittle on my cheeks. That mission may have been a simulation, but the panel's verdict was real enough: Andy Bustamante was unfit to be a case officer. My ego got the better of me that day. I thought I'd made myself untouchable, and that was what made me sloppy. This time, I was playing for keeps. I could not let that happen again.

So now a different thought spread through my mind like a bloodstain through a crisp white shirt. *They don't need eyes on you to know where you are. You know this. They can track your phone, turn on its microphone and cameras remotely. They can use closed-circuit cameras, just like the ones at Kestrel Airport. They can use drones, some too small or too high up for you to see. Thinking they are not watching is wishful thinking—dangerous wishful thinking. So stay alert.*

Snow was falling again. It gathered on top of yesterday's slush, refracting the soot stains and turning everything shades of gray. I gathered my coat around me and made for the sedan.

"Mister Hernandez?" said the driver.

The car smelled nice: evidently the Doe Company wanted to make a good impression on Alex Hernandez. Unlike the surly airport cabbies, this driver was attentive and chatty.

"Where are you from? Is this your first time in Kestrel?"

I had no choice but to engage in small talk: it was what they would expect from an American. If this driver was reporting to somebody, as he surely was, silence from the back seat might alert them. But while chatting, I had to remain vigilant. I squeezed myself into one corner, pressing my face as close as possible to the window, while still trying to look relaxed. I was by no means sure, but as we drove I saw maybe five vehicles that might have been following us. I committed them all to memory.

After about thirty minutes on the highway, the car pulled up to a pair of squat buildings behind a chain-link fence. My contact, the eponymous Mr. Doe, was waiting by the door. Our first order of business was a tour of his facility. It was just after 8 a.m., but already row after row of people in identical blue boiler suits and hairnets were standing at metal workbenches, working for low pay. The plant smelled of petroleum and hot metal.

"This widget comes from Europe," Mr. Doe said, gesturing toward a thicket of plastic tubes and steel cylinders. "That one is from Asia.

These are the best in the world." He spoke with pride about their weekly production, monthly goals, and yearly ambitions. If necessary, he said, they would run twenty-four-hour shifts to meet demand. Looking at the workers as they toiled away amid the heat and noise and grime, I didn't doubt it.

Mr. Doe took me to an adjacent building, which housed the main admin offices. The boardroom doubled as a supply closet, with boxes of hairnets, gloves, and stationery piled up on the floor and on one end of the conference table. Doe talked me through the company's international sales numbers. Frankly (putting Alex Hernandez's executive hat on for a moment), I was not convinced that such a small firm could deliver the required volume, let alone scale alongside Acme's plans for aggressive expansion. But I promised Mr. Doe a response within the week.

"Thank you, Mister Hernandez," said Mr. Doe. "If you wish, the driver will take you to your next appointment."

I thanked Mr. Doe and asked to be taken to the café I was due to case for Tasha. Again, I sat diagonally in the back seat, eyes peeled for anything unusual. The highway crawled by. Cars jostled for position amid the traffic.

Nothing.

Nothing.

*Wait.*

That gray sedan. Hadn't I seen it before? Outwardly, the gray sedan was bland—suspiciously bland. It was the same color as the polluted snow. There was no bumper sticker. No Nikes up on the dash. No kitschy doodad dangling from the rearview mirror. It wasn't speeding or weaving impatiently or doing any of the things normal drivers did. In fact, it seemed to hang back, weaving in and out of traffic like a shark, staying always exactly two cars behind. After a few minutes, the gray sedan exited, and its place was taken up by a white sedan. I was pretty sure I'd seen that one before, too. The same went for the blue sedan that replaced it, in turn.

That made three of the five potentials I had seen on the first leg of my journey. If these cars really were following me—and I still wasn't sure they were—there was only one way they could have picked up the trail so far from my hotel: they must have been tracking my cell phone.

At this point, an amateur would react by throwing away the cell phone like an apple with a worm in it. But if you are really being tailed, that is hands down the worst thing you can do.

When Hollywood depicts secret agents or undercover cops being tracked through a city, it's usually a fast-paced game of hide-and-seek in which the agent has to stay out of sight of the big bad enemy. I won't say that's never the case—just *almost* never. In fact, it's usually the exact opposite. For the most part, you want your tail to be able to see you as much as possible. Why? Because a surveillance team that loses sight of you is apt to assume you are attempting escape, at which point they call in their much less pleasant colleagues, the capture squad.

Imagine you are walking through the woods alone and you notice a bear emerging from the trees. You see its teeth. You see its claws. Your every instinct is to run, but that's the worst thing you can do. If you run, you will only provoke the bear to give chase. So instead, you move slowly. You have to make the bear think you are not afraid of it, no matter how much you might be sweating and trembling. Gradually you back away. "Lulling surveillance" is what we call the technique.

That's not to say that it's never time to run. If the bear does charge, running might be your only option. But I was still pretty far from that point, right?

\* \* \*

The café was three two-story buildings surrounding a central walled courtyard. Traditionally, these courtyard dwellings house three generations of the same relatively well-off family, but this one was converted: one of the buildings had become a kitchen, while the other two housed a seating area for about seventy-five customers. The surrounding neighborhood was mostly residential, quieter during the day than a shopping district, which made it easier to detect surveillance.

As a lover of Falconian baked goods, I had been looking forward to this visit since I began planning for the trip. I pictured myself spending about an hour here, enjoying the freshly baked cakes, the scent of which was now filling my nostrils. But in light of my suspicions about surveillance, my plans were changing rapidly. I ate the cake in a hurry and ordered hot coffee to go.

As usual, I planned my routes through Kestrel according to the acronym PACE—primary, alternate, contingency, emergency—used by military operators throughout the US. Only the last of these would involve abandoning all pretense of cover consistency and simply running for the exit (in this case, Kestrel Airport). The other three were the different routes I would follow through the city, depending on the circumstances.

In view of the surveillance vehicles I thought I had seen, I now moved to my alternate route. I would walk through a residential neighborhood to another point on my map, a little store that James had identified on a prior visit. It was a good spot because it was in a quiet neighborhood with not much else going on, but that alone would not be enough. Going to such a store just to buy, say, a pack of cigarettes would be suspicious: why not get your smokes from any one of ten thousand other, more accessible stores selling the same products?

What made this particular store such a find was the rarity of some of its merchandise. The owner was an immigrant to Falcon, and about once a year he received a shipping container full of mixed merchandise from his homeland. If you owned a certain model of European cell phone, for example, this was plausibly the only place in town that would stock a spare battery. And it just so happened that Alex Hernandez owned such a brand of cell phone.

I turned the corner and stepped into a lane lined with sheds propped against the walls of more prosperous houses. These lanes are too narrow for cars to drive down, and that was exactly how I wanted it: to force any surveillants, if that was what they were, to exit their vehicles and follow me on foot. That way, I could get a good look at them. At the same time, I was careful not to rush: remember, the worst thing you can do is make the bear chase you.

I strolled down several more lanes, holding my coffee up to my nose as people often do in Kestrel to block out the stench of the city.

Locals hurried past me. The locals in Kestrel generally did everything faster than Americans would. But when turning a corner (deliberately incorporated into my route), I glanced back for a moment and spotted a single exception: a man in a hat with ear flaps. The hat reminded me of Sherlock Holmes, so that was the nickname I gave him. Instead of overtaking me like everyone else, Sherlock studiously matched my pace, staying a fixed distance behind me, just as the storm-gray sedan had done on the highway.

A bell went *ting-a-ling* as I entered the store. The old proprietor gave me a brown-toothed smile. "Ah yes!" said the man.

I held up my to-go cup in salutation and returned the grin. "Hot coffee for a cold day!" I said in English.

"Ha, yes! Good coffee! Please!" He indicated his modest store, which smelled of plastic wrap and dust. What I was most aware of, although I only dared look at it with my peripheral vision, was the closed-circuit camera high up on the wall. If Falcon intelligence were indeed following me, they would certainly pull the footage after I left. They would also no doubt question the shop owner, so I had to be on my best behavior. Meaning that everything had to look nice and natural, without any obvious stalling for time.

The place was stacked floor-to-ceiling with knockoff goods: everything from Fony headphones to Spintendo backpacks. You really had to hunt for what you needed. *Good,* I thought. *It will give them time to change the eye.* If he really was a sophisticated operative, Sherlock would be radioing right now to request a handover while I was occupied inside the store. Give the other car about two minutes to find some place to pull over. Allow another three minutes to get the new eye in place and let Sherlock get back to his car. I wanted them to have plenty of time to do this because (a) it would keep the surveillance team nice and relaxed; and (b) if they changed the eye, I would get a look at a second surveillant. I would give them at least five minutes before I emerged from the store.

I found the phone battery more quickly than I expected—too quickly, in fact. Damn. When did this place get so organized? I had to give the team more time, without letting the CCTV camera see me stalling. Think fast: *What else could I get?*

I thought of my local language teacher back in Wolf, who always had little trinkets dangling from her cell phone. Maybe Alex Hernandez's fiancée was a woman like her? This turned out to be perfect. There were a lot of little tassels and crystals to sort through, and Alex Hernandez wouldn't know exactly what to get. I took my time selecting one to fit the personality I had just constructed in my head: a little sparkly charm.

As I left the store with my purchases in hand, I told myself: *If I see Sherlock again, he's the usual bumbling minder. If I see someone else, I'm in trouble.*

Outside, there was no sign of Sherlock.

*Shit.*

But there, catty-corner from the store, stood another man, sporting a shiny nylon bomber jacket. Unlike everyone else on the street, Bomberman was just standing there, loitering. Other than that, he was a better fit for this neighborhood than Sherlock: a smart choice by his team leader.

*Shit, shit.*

It was now about ten thirty—time for Alex Hernandez to head across town to his second meeting. I headed for a main road to hail a cab. And sure enough, just like his colleague before him, Bomberman tailed me at a fixed distance.

*Shit, shit, shit.*

At least now I knew what I was up against. The technical name for this kind of operation, as used by law enforcement and private eyes, is discreet-to-lose surveillance. Meaning that they would watch, hang back, even risk losing sight of their prey, all in order to remain concealed. It's one of the most sophisticated forms of surveillance that exists. Discreet-to-lose teams usually comprise five vehicles: four civilian cars plus a command vehicle, typically a van bristling with antennae. There would be two agents in each car, plus up to seven in the van, for a grand total of perhaps fifteen agents—more than double the total staff of the Cell. Not the kind of resources they would waste on mild-mannered businessman Alex Hernandez. Which meant that they knew, or at least suspected, that Alex was not really Alex.

*Is this the mole at work?* I wondered. *Has he unmasked me? Did I screw up somehow, just like I did on the Farm?*

The cab crawled through Kestrel's never-ending traffic. My stomach did backflips as I watched the white sedan and the blue sedan take turns tailing me. I told myself that I had at least one thing on my side:

even Falcon intelligence, bold and brutal as they were, would not arrest an American citizen for espionage without substantial evidence, for the simple reason that to do so would, by definition, cause a diplomatic incident, and diplomatic incidents were very bad for business. If worse came to worst, the United States could theoretically impose trade or financial sanctions on Falcon.

Moreover, Falcon officials couldn't cite the mole's say-so as evidence against Alex, either, because that would be to admit publicly that they had a mole, which would create a worse foreign-policy rift. So the surveillance team's objective would be to gather incriminating evidence against me. Only then would they close in and make the arrest. All I had to do was deny them the pleasure of a pretext.

Unless...

*Shit, shit, shit, shit.*

Unless they already *had* the evidence and were just waiting for an opportune moment to strike. My throat went dry. My coat, which had felt like protective armor back at the hotel, suddenly became uncomfortably hot and constrictive. Inside the heavy gloves, sweat pricked my palms. Already, I seemed to feel the cable ties around my wrists and ankles, the black bag over my head. I would be taken to a prison somewhere, starved, deprived of sleep, squeezed for all the information I could give. Maybe then I would be put on public display as a propaganda tool — if I was lucky, that is. If not, I would simply disappear into the Falcon prison system to waste away slowly from malnutrition or else be shot while attempting to escape. People went missing all the time in Falcon — locals, foreigners, businessmen, spies. One more would barely be noticed.

I thought about Jihi. We'd been married just a few years. Would we ever see each other again? What would life be like for her, effectively a widow even while her husband was still alive in some squalid prison cell? Or worse, what if she had to spend the rest of her life not knowing whether I was alive or dead? I could hardly bear to think of her going through that.

And yet, I knew that I must not try to flee. That would only invite capture, and in a country so heavily watched, it would almost certainly not work. The only thing to do was to avoid, to the best of my ability, giving the Falconers any opening to descend upon me. Above all, that meant staying as true as possible to the character of sensible, level-headed Alex Hernandez.

*You are trained for this,* I told myself, over and over. *Do not run. Do not run.*

My second appointment of the day was at Kestrel Supply Corporation, which turned out to be a much larger and more established group than the young and scrappy Doe Company. Alex Hernandez's contact, Mr. Smith, spoke better English and knew US etiquette—the handshakes, the small talk, the mutual ass-kissing—better than Mr. Doe did. His suit was more expensive and better pressed. Here, there was no tour. The main production facility was somewhere else. This was just the corporate headquarters, which on its own was larger than the Doe Company's whole complex. Scalability would not be a problem for Acme if we went with Kestrel Supply Corporation. Even the air smelled better—as in my hotel, it was perfumed with a fresh fabric scent. Yet—and here was the catch—the classier nature of the operation was reflected in the price Mr. Smith quoted across the polished wood of the conference table.

A savvy businessman like Alex Hernandez would see that he was presented with two bad options: one cheap but unscalable, the other scalable but expensive. Alex had a third meeting planned for tomorrow.

If I were to stay strictly in character, I would surely attend that meeting and take another shot at getting a workable quote. Alex Hernandez would stay—there was no reason not to. But what about Andy Bustamante? My instinct told me to catch the next flight out of Kestrel. Such a blatant break in character would be risky. On the other hand, sticking around might prove even more dangerous.

I had a decision to make, and it could mean freedom or captivity—even life or death.

I want to note, at this point, yet another difference between the movies and real life. James Bond and Ethan Hunt are often shown wearing earpieces and concealed microphones, and their whereabouts are tracked constantly by their handlers in London or Langley, who can communicate directly with them in real time. But reality is not like that, and it's worth taking a moment to understand why.

First off, it would be far too conspicuous. An intelligence officer walking around talking to themselves—or worse, into their sleeve or lapel—would risk getting arrested on the spot. Even if nobody actually saw you using it, signal traffic to and from the tech could easily be detected. More likely, you would never get to that point, because the wire would be discovered in airport bag screenings.

Besides—and here's the real clincher—the cost of staffing a twenty-four-hour ops center to track every field operative in real time would blow CIA's annual budget in about half a day, along with the director's career. After that, good luck persuading Congress to appropriate more funds.

Bottom line: when in the field, you are on your own. Here in the Falcon capital, surrounded by inquisitive eyes and ears, there was no backup. No mythic evac chopper waiting to pick me up. The hidden earpieces, the friendly satellites tracking an agent's every move, the team back at base guiding you in real time—those things are Hollywood's purview, not Langley's. As an undercover CIA operative on hostile ground, I had nothing but my wits, my training, and my prayers.

In other words, whatever path I chose, the decision was mine and mine alone.

I needed to buy some time to think it through.

Mr. Smith, like Mr. Doe before him, had a car waiting to take Alex Hernandez wherever he might be headed next. But in the doorway of the Kestrel Supply Corporation, I stalled, examining the proffered business card line by line.

Mr. Smith looked at me as if to say, "Why are you still here? I got shit to do, man." But the fact was, I needed this little piece of theater to give the surveillance team time to stub their cigarettes, scramble back to their cars, and get ready to follow me. Once again, the most dangerous thing is a flustered tail. So move slowly. Keep the bear calm.

By this time, I had abandoned my alternate plan and escalated to stage three of PACE: the contingency. Once in the car, I asked to be taken to the tourist district, Kestrel's equivalent of Times Square. The area would be packed with people. Usually, that's not ideal: too many eyes. But at this stage, the crowds would make it more difficult to execute an arrest, if that was what they had in mind. If things got any worse, I might have to abandon the contingency plan, too, and activate the emergency—in other words, run. If it did come to that, a crowd might make it easier for me to slip away, too.

On the drive over, I thought I caught glimpses of the storm-gray and dark-blue cars trailing us. There was no sign of a white sedan. Evidently, they were swapping the vehicles in and out on a regular rotation: another staple of discreet-to-lose surveillance.

As I exited my cab in the bustling square, I saw, out of the corner of my eye, a fourth vehicle pulling over, maybe three car-lengths ahead. This one was a red compact SUV. I hadn't seen it before, but I paid attention to the passenger who got out: a middle-aged woman in a checked jacket and earmuffs. Women, I knew, were rare among Falcon intelligence officers (female civilians cajoled into becoming honey-traps were a different matter). So was Earmuffs really part of the team? Or was I just growing paranoid? The idea that I might not be thinking straight was a worrying sign in itself. More than ever, I needed space to clear my head.

Here in the tourist quarter of Kestrel, the buildings gleamed. It was deliberately done for the benefit of visiting foreigners, the product of frequent power-washing that kept each façade clean of soot and grime. I headed for a fairly fancy restaurant that I had visited before as Alex Hernandez. It was on the second floor, overlooking the street, so it offered a decent vantage point. Once inside, I inverted the usual rule of intelligence by turning my back to the body of the restaurant, and faced the big windows.

"See?" I wanted to signal to my surveillants. "A spy would never sit here, offering his back to you. I'm no spy, I'm just plain old Alex Hernandez, out for lunch. Nothing to get agitated about. I'm nobody. Nothing worth eating here, bear. Go hibernate."

After a few minutes, another patron was seated at the table immediately behind me—someone who, like me, came in alone. If it was a surveillant—and I was pretty sure it was—this was another escalation. Putting an officer that close to his target represents a huge risk—one they wouldn't take if all they wanted was to steal business trade secrets or whatever. When they get that close, they are watching for your local contact coming in the door. If you exchange something—a SIM card, a USB stick—they want to be near enough to observe that happening.

Well, I wasn't going to give them that satisfaction. Thanks to the cell model, I wouldn't be meeting any intelligence sources or exchanging any data—we left that up to the case officers. I was going to look as squeaky-clean as possible, just like the boring mid-level executive I was pretending to be.

Above all, I could not afford to look like I had surveillance-detection training. *Don't look behind you,* I told myself. Making eye contact is one of the most dangerous things you can do: it confirms that you know they are following you. Just like with a wild animal, it's perceived as aggressive. So I took my time with lunch, forcing myself to look out the window instead of behind me at what might well be one of the surveillance team.

Was it Sherlock? Bomberman? Earmuffs? *Don't look.*

I slurped my soup and sipped my coffee and took stock of my predicament. I had spotted multiple surveillants and multiple cars. One of the potential watchers was female, which suggested a specialist team. Plus, whoever was at the table behind me had moved in close enough to see who I might be meeting with—something they would only do if they thought they were dealing with a trained intel officer.

I reminded myself that this was only day one of a three-day trip. From my training in Falcon counterintelligence methods, I knew all too well how it would develop from here. Five vehicles on day one would grow to seven, with a drone tracking my cell phone signal on day two. On day three, there would be nine vehicles—and one of those would be a panel van with a SWAT team waiting inside to take me in. Sticking around until that happened was not an option. I needed to get out, but—crucially—without alarming the bear.

Going directly to the airport, after less than twenty-four hours in Falcon, would trigger alarm bells. Waiting until day three was too dangerous. But maybe there was a middle path? Alex Hernandez could email Acme with a supplier update and get put on a flight first thing tomorrow. That wouldn't be too suspicious, right? If questioned, I could say that I loved Mr. Doe's moxie so much that I decided to go with him, the scrappy underdog, without even going to the third meeting. I was excited to get started with Doe, that was all. Strike while the iron is hot and yadda yadda. Pretty thin, but it was the best I could do. So it was settled: Alex Hernandez, unimportant middle-management nobody, decided to leave tomorrow morning.

Until then, I wanted nothing more than to return to my hotel and hide out. But I wouldn't be safe there, either. In fact, the relative tranquility of the hotel might give the Falconers a better opportunity to make the arrest, if that was where this was heading. Besides, knowing for sure there was a surveillance team on me, I now owed a duty to my fellow members of the Cell: I had to get eyes on as many members of this rival counterintelligence team as possible, for as long as possible. With their physical descriptions in hand, I could alert James, Tasha, Beverly, and Luke to be on their guard. If they saw even one of those faces, they would know it was time to run.

I finished my food, paid the check in cash, and got up to leave. The diner at the table behind me stayed, but his face was a new one: a young guy, mid-twenties, in designer athletic wear, the word PUMA emblazoned across his chest. He ordered an appetizer and a Coke and barely touched either during the entire time it took me to eat my lunch, and I was taking my time over it. Puma had a phone, but the screen was off. He was trying, albeit not very effectively, to hide his face behind his hand: surveillants don't want to make eye contact either.

I committed Puma's description to memory and began to think of other places where I could draw the surveillance team close. But first, there was something else I had to do.

## JIHI

I was having lunch with some Agency colleagues in "food alley" behind our office building when my phone rang. Not my regular phone: the crummy burner phone Andy and I bought as part of our home-brew commo plan. CIA couldn't have my "real" number finding its way into the Falcon intelligence data lake.

"Hey, my love," Andy said. No names: that was deliberate.

"Oh, hey," I said, slurping a noodle. "How's your trip?"

"Good, good. Actually, I might be a bit ahead of schedule here. I'm going to talk to Josh and Liz about maybe coming home early."

At that, my heart lurched. Everyone at CIA knew that "coming home early" from an operation could not be good.

Worst-case scenarios crowded my mind. I saw Andy in a Falcon prison. I remembered the captured case officers we learned about in basic. They were often held incommunicado to begin with. Sometimes, by the time Langley realized they were still alive, it was too late.

I knew I couldn't give voice to any of this. I couldn't even offer reassurance, because whoever might be listening in would wonder why Alex Hernandez needed reassurance. Just as much as Andy was undercover as Alex, right now I was undercover as Alex's fiancée.

"Okay babe. Good news! Can't wait to see you."

"Love you. See you soon."

I finished my lunch in silence, pretending to be deep in thought about something else.

"Is everything all right?" somebody asked.

"It's fine," I said. "I got something kind of concerning, and... You know what? I'll figure it out." I used the tone of voice we use when we don't want further questions. We were out in public, and even CIA colleagues could be suspect — after all, we were in this mess because of a mole.

On the inside, however, my thoughts were spiraling out of control. I imagined Andy being rolled up by Falcon intelligence exactly the way they trained us for: a vanload of thugs, a bag over his head, cable ties around his wrists and ankles. Protocol dictated that CIA would say nothing. The US government would insist that Alex Hernandez was an ordinary person with no intelligence ties, and that this was all a case of mistaken identity. They would want this to go away as quickly as possible. I would be left beating down doors to get anything done about his case. Or, even worse: he would just vanish and we'd never know if he was alive or dead.

After locking my cell phone away in the signal-blocking security box, I made a beeline for James's office. As one of the cocreators of the Cell, James needed to know. And as a Falcon House hand, he had more access to information than I did. He might know why Andy was coming home early.

Full of nervous energy, I blurted out my worst fears to James. He let me talk. After I finished, there was a long pause while James digested the information.

He said he'd seen no indication of anything untoward in Kestrel. "I'm sure Andy's fine," he said. I reminded myself that not too long ago, James had spent three weeks squatting in a hut waiting to meet with Evade. He knew what not-fine looked like. So if James thought things were fine, that was a good sign, right?

To begin with, I took comfort in that. But later, I realized that James's reassurance, however sincerely meant, was hollow: he didn't know what was going on any more than I did.

Back in my own office, I scrubbed through classified emails and cable traffic, searching for some innocuous reason that might have prompted Andy to leave Kestrel early. It's the same impulse people get when they hear a big boom outside: start scrolling through news sites and social media to find out what happened. But deep down, I knew I would come up empty—this endless scrolling was just something to do, to keep my mind occupied. To keep me from screaming into the void.

My office mate, Leah, came in. I must have looked like a crazy person, because she immediately asked me what was wrong. Leah was a case officer working local targets in and around Wolf. Her husband, Hank, was also a CIA officer as well as a hard-as-nails former Marine aviator. Both had served in active war zones, and between them, it was safe to say, Leah and Hank had seen it all. It helped, too, that Leah was bubbly, friendly, and whip-smart—the intelligence equivalent of Elle from *Legally Blonde*. Folks from all over the office would come to her for advice and to talk through their feelings. Usually, she made everyone feel better. But even Leah wasn't clued in on Cell business, so I had to keep it vague.

"Oh my God, Leah," I whispered. "Andy is coming home early."

Leah inhaled sharply. She knew enough about our work to know this was not good news. "Okay, Jihi. Breathe. Don't worry. Maybe…" Leah forced a grin. "Maybe he just pissed the local station off so bad they kicked him out?"

This type of thing does happen, usually in party towns where wayward officers sometimes get drunk and start fights. But "party town" does not describe the grim city of Kestrel. Moreover, while Andy could be impulsive, he was not reckless enough to allow something like that to happen during a mission.

"Okay, okay," Leah said, seeing my face. "Bad joke. I'm sorry. Look, bottom line: the case officers out there won't let anything bad happen to him."

Again, this was not reassuring. The case officers in Kestrel would know Andy was there, but they wouldn't know where in the city he was operating. Any contact between Andy and the local station would jeopardize everyone concerned.

Leah tried to make up for her bad joke by telling a story about a time Hank went missing in a war zone after a huge explosion. She heard nothing from him for hours. "I was sure he had died," Leah said. She'd gotten herself into a panic, thinking he was caught up in a "green-on-blue" attack—one of those horrific incidents where a US contact blew themselves up, taking Americans with them.

"But later," Leah said, "he showed up again saying, 'It was just a suicide bomber. It was five clicks away,' or whatever. You know how military types talk. If Hank can survive that, Andy can get through this. Don't worry."

"I guess so," I said. But I remembered that Hank was the guy who once told us how if you are shipwrecked you can drink turtle blood for nutrition. So maybe his survival skills were a notch or two higher than Andy's.

Turning back to my computer screen, I shook my head vigorously, trying to dislodge the terrors swirling around in there. "There's no point in worrying about it," I told myself. "You can't change it. Besides, you have work to do. You and Andy built the Cell together. Andy would want you to carry on with the mission. Get back to it, girl!"

This is another reason why CIA likes intramural couples: when one is away, especially in a dangerous place, the other tends to respond by throwing themselves into their work. From the Agency's perspective, it's very efficient.

As I pored over reams of targeting data, searching for the telltale patterns that would lead to more Cell contacts, a little voice in the back of my head kept reminding me that I had married a misfit—a man whose overconfidence on the Farm got him forever barred from fulfilling his dream of becoming a case officer. But Andy had learned his lesson from that episode, hadn't he? *Surely,* I thought, *he will not run unnecessary risks.*

## ANDY

I hadn't expected to get through to Jihi. When we were in the office, our phones had to be locked up in the "vault," an electromagnetically sealed box. It was just luck that she happened to be having lunch when I called. I found it reassuring to hear her voice. As we spoke, all the hubbub of Kestrel's tourist district seemed to slip into soft focus. On any other day, I would have loved to give all my attention to my wife— we did that all the time on our mini-dates around campus at Langley. But here in this hostile city, any lapse in concentration could be fatal. I needed my wits about me if I was going to make it through the next eighteen hours. So I cut the conversation short with a curt "See you soon," as if by saying it out loud I could make it so.

Like Jihi, I dealt with the stress of the situation by focusing on the task at hand: collecting as much information as possible on the opposing cell. To do that, I would need to entice them even closer. I saw the perfect place to do so: a large bookstore. Places like this, with ample hiding spots between row upon row of shelves, are popular locations for spy meetings. If it's too conspicuous to meet up in person, you can find an unpopular book and slip a coded message in at page 325 or whatever.

Alex Hernandez didn't read Falconian (nor, for the most part, do I), so I headed for the English language section, where I discovered a little subsection devoted to memoir. Incongruously, I found myself reading a biography of Benjamin Franklin — an odd thing to find in a country so fiercely committed to the opposite of the democratic freedoms for which Franklin stood. Glancing up, whom should I see but Earmuffs — the middle-aged woman in the checked jacket who was at the drop-off fully ninety minutes before. I had doubted that she was even a member of the surveillance squad, but now there she was in the self-help section, pretending to read *The Seven Habits of Highly Effective People.*

*Gotcha,* I thought. With furtive glances, taking care to avoid eye contact, I drank in Earmuffs's appearance, storing her face and demeanor in my memory. That done, I put the Ben Franklin book back on the shelf and headed out. Earmuffs would check the book for notes and come up empty. See? This guy's no spy. You're wasting your time.

I could feel my confidence coming back. I was good at this, after all. James had said so. Experience was confirming it. The other members of the Cell looked to me for guidance. Well, I'd be returning from this trip with a full rogue's gallery of the people chasing us: Cell one, Falcon intelligence zero.

Having confirmed Earmuffs as a member of the surveillance cell tailing me, I now wanted to confirm the young guy from the restaurant, Puma. I needed a place Alex Hernandez could credibly go where it would make sense to send Puma, a young man, but *not* Earmuffs, a middle-aged woman. I soon found what I thought would be the perfect spot: a huge video arcade. Four floors of bleeping, blasting, and blinking lights. Alex was kind of bored after two business meetings and a sleepy old bookshop, right? He was craving some cheap thrills.

Inside, the arcade stank of sweat and fried food. I took my time buying tokens—again in cash, no paper trails—and browsing the arcade cabinets on the ground floor. About five minutes, I reckoned, would be enough time for whoever is controlling the rival team to order Puma into the arcade.

*Let's get a good look at you,* I thought, my confidence growing. I sought out a game I could play while still keeping an eye on my surroundings. On the second floor, I found a dinosaur-hunting game where you stood back from the cabinet and attempted to dead-eye T. Rexes with a blue plastic AK-47. This was ideal, so long as I didn't look like too good of a shot. I hunted dinos with childish zeal, reliving my past life as a gamer, pre-Agency. Meanwhile, in my peripheral vision, I scanned for signs of Puma.

I squinted down the barrel of the plastic rifle. The T. Rex was looking right at me, clawing at the dirt with its hind leg. I had a good, clean shot at it. My finger hovered over the trigger.

At that moment, a figure appeared around the right-hand side of the arcade cabinet, little more than two arms' breadths away. It was someone I recognized from earlier in the day. But it wasn't Puma. It was Bomberman, the guy from outside the knockoff shop, hours ago and miles across town.

In the confusion of that moment, there was no time to calibrate my reactions. We locked eyes, each of us visibly recognizing the other. My heart stopped. I had been made. Now they knew for sure that I had intelligence training.

Bomberman's mouth hung open. On impulse, I squeezed the blue plastic trigger. My shot went wide. The T. Rex roared and charged me. Its jaws clamped shut and blood-red text filled the screen.

GAME OVER.

## JIHI

My afternoon crawled by. Nobody called with news. There was nothing in the cables, nothing in the official emails, nothing in the secure chat, no matter how many times I refreshed them. I couldn't check the burner phone Andy and I had bought, or the email account we had set up. Those were strictly for the private commo plan we had established between ourselves. Neither was cleared for use inside the office. I felt like an antsy schoolkid again, desperate for the bell to ring so I could get out of there.

Toward the end of the workday, James ducked in to tell me he'd seen nothing on the channels he had access to.

"But that's a good thing," James added hastily. "No news is good news, right?"

As early as I dared, I dashed out the door. On a normal day, I would have walked back through the city to our apartment. Today, I hailed a cab so I could get to my private computer faster. I checked the burner phone on the way, switching it on and off in case there was something wrong with it. When I got home, I opened my personal laptop. There was nothing in the email account either, but that didn't stop me refreshing the page a billion times just in case.

James had said no news was good news. But if Andy hadn't been kicked out by the local office, then that must mean —

*Stop,* I told myself. *This is not healthy. He's fine. He knows what to do. We have a commo plan, and it hasn't even been eight hours, let alone twenty-four. He'll be in touch. And there's nothing you can do about it right now anyway.*

I forced myself to shut the laptop and put the cell phone away. I went to the gym early and set the treadmill way faster than normal. Back home, my thighs aching, I binged on ice cream and crappy TV. I did what I could to stay sane. But my mind kept coming back to the image of Andy starving in a prison camp.

"Please, please, let him be okay," I said into the void.

## ANDY

With a dead weight in my stomach, I realized that choosing the arcade was a mistake. It was too loud for radio communications. Too dark and too crowded for my tails to keep me in their line of sight. The surveillance team lost me, forcing them to execute what we call a starburst: sending every available officer out at once to hunt me down. Ordinarily, Bomberman would have changed clothes before being sent after me a second time, but here he was in the same outfit, suggesting that the team had panicked.

Espionage is like chess: winning is about making fewer wrong moves than your opponent. And I had just made the worst wrong move of my life: I made them feel like they were losing me. Instead of lulling the bear, I provoked it. It smelled my blood. I'd gotten cocky again, like in training, and now I was about to pay for it for real.

After what felt like an eternity, Bomberman broke eye contact and glided out of my line of sight. With a trembling hand, I holstered the blue plastic rifle.

I knew what came next. Right now, Bomberman was heading outside to radio the command vehicle. "The target made me," he was saying. "Requesting immediate apprehension." The surveillance team would be pulling back to let the snatch squad move in.

In training, they subject you to elements of arrest. They show you what the zip ties will feel like when they tighten around your wrists; what it's like to have a bag pulled over your head and feel it clog your breathing; how they will jerk your hands behind your back when they force you to walk. But those experiences, however unpleasant, could not compare to the real thing. In the simulations, the bag on my head smelled of Tide, not blood or vomit. The zip ties were new, not worn and jagged against the thin skin of my wrists. Nobody body-slammed me onto the hood of a car, or dragged my face across the asphalt, or dislocated my shoulder as they bundled me into a vehicle, or broke my nose against the floor of a black panel van.

In a trance, I gravitated to the most mindless game I could find on that floor of the arcade: a demolition derby where you gained points by deliberately crashing your car into other vehicles. While I played, I deployed certain emotion-handling techniques I had learned on the Farm.

It's not that I was trying to suppress my feelings entirely: you need emotions like fear and excitement to tell you when things aren't right, and to spur you on to take action. It's more like cooking with oil. A canny chef knows that when the oil starts to smoke, it's time to turn the heat down. Langley trains you to detect that smoke and dial things back appropriately.

On one occasion, I was meeting a roleplaying contact in a hotel room when a SWAT team blasted the door down and held us at gunpoint, barking accusations. Later, I was driving on a closed course when another vehicle screamed up behind me and started ramming my car. Later still, I was presented with four of my buddies lying on the ground covered in blood. I had to triage them while the instructors yelled, "He's got forty-five seconds before he bleeds out! Do something!"

In situations like that, you don't have time to remember that it's just an exercise. A large part of the reason we're put through these ordeals is to feel the spike of adrenaline and cortisol, to learn from the inside what happens when a human amygdala—the brain's seat of emotions—gets overwhelmed. You become foggy, disoriented. Your reasoning is impaired.

When you get into a state like that, you learn to run through a series of physiological processes. You slow your breathing to bring your heart rate down and decrease your blood pressure. One good routine is box breathing, where you breathe in for four seconds, hold it for four, breathe out for four, hold it for four, and repeat. You don't tell yourself not to freak out—that would only make you panic more. Instead, you give the fear centers of your brain time and space to flare up…and flame out. You mentally let the panic process happen while you concentrate on breathing. Your goal is to wait out the fear and panic until the logical part of your brain can catch up. After that, you can start to analyze the situation properly and come up with a plan.

The most pressing question was: should I try to run? If so, I would need to change my appearance and my digital signature. Looking along the rows of arcade cabinets, I saw how easy it would be to steal a jacket, a hat, a phone from the piles of personal belongings dumped on chairs or slung over railings while their owners engrossed themselves in the games. Undercover operatives of all kinds are trained in petty theft for exactly these circumstances, except we don't call it stealing. We call it procurement. Next, I would find the back exit—the one least likely to be covered by a squad. Outside, I would steal a motorbike and tear off, weaving through traffic to evade my pursuers.

If I ran, where would I go? Not to any Agency facility—that would blow it wide open, endangering many more lives than just my own. Not to the US embassy, either. There's far too much security in the diplomatic quarter, as anyone who has visited Embassy Row in Washington, DC, will have seen firsthand. Even if you did make it inside, what would you do? Live there forever? At the very least, you would spark a diplomatic confrontation between the United States and Falcon. Intelligence officers work in the shadows in order to reduce open hostility, not increase it.

So if I were to run, I would be running for an exit. Which one? A seaport would have the least security, but booking passage on a vessel could take days. Leaving overland, by train or car, could work, but the length of the journey would give the authorities plenty of time to flag my passport and have me stopped at the border. The only viable option was the quickest: the airport. Get there as soon as possible, and jump on the next flight, anywhere but here. Yet the airport was also the option with the tightest security and the most opportunities to have me arrested, assuming word reached the border protection service in time.

By this point, I had been playing the demolition derby game for a few minutes. The hood of my car was crumpled and smoking. But thanks to the breathing exercises, my mind was clear. If I ran, I'd most likely be caught. And it would be worse for me, because I would have stolen property right out in the open—more than enough, under Falcon law, to justify holding me pretty much indefinitely as a common thief.

So it came down to this: my best option, my only option, was to continue my day as Alex Hernandez, behaving as normally as possible. In a few minutes, I would leave the arcade. If I got arrested, as I feared and suspected I would, then throughout the inevitable interrogation to follow I would take the same tack as I had in the Major Bondoy training exercise: stick rigidly to my cover story, no matter how flimsy it might become, and no matter how much pressure the Falconers might apply. It might not save me, in the end—but it would avoid making a bad situation even worse: as they teach us in training, self-confessed spies receive even harsher treatment than suspected ones.

I took a deep breath, clambered out from behind the plastic steering wheel, and headed for the main exit. Out on the street, an ocean of faces engulfed me: locals, tourists, police. I walked around the tourist district, keeping my movements steady and deliberate, bracing for the command van, the SWAT team, the cable ties cutting into my wrists. For an hour, I window-shopped, bought snacks and cups of coffee, took in the sights, and generally behaved as innocent, everyday Alex Hernandez would. I saw nothing. The surveillance team had pulled back, but the arrest team had not yet moved in. Most likely they were waiting until I took myself to a quieter place. Civilians would only get in the way, and besides, no intelligence officer wants to draw unnecessary attention to themselves. But I couldn't melt into the crowd forever.

After an hour or so of play-acting as a tourist, I forced myself to walk toward the local taxi stand. I didn't jostle or fight for a cab the way the locals always did. I was on my best behavior now, and I had to avoid offering the Falconers any pretext for a confrontation. Besides, I wasn't in a hurry to get to a neighborhood where arresting me might prove easier. Finally, a cab opened up. I asked to be taken to a shopping square near my hotel.

Rush hour was just beginning, but already the traffic crawled. The cabbie had the heating on full-blast against the winter cold, making the back seat feel like a pressure cooker. Twisting my body around inside my heavy coat, I saw a familiar car behind us. It was the dark-blue late-model sedan, and this time, I saw the occupants. In the passenger seat sat Earmuffs. The driver I recognized as Sherlock, the man with the ear-flapped hat who was the first surveillant I had identified that morning.

With that, I felt my panic subside a little. If the surveillance team was still on my case, it meant the arrest team was not — or at least, not right now. But, I reminded myself, that didn't change the fact that

Bomberman had seen me recognize him. So this reprieve was most likely only temporary.

Assuming I stuck to my new plan to take the red-eye out of Kestrel the next morning, I could think of at least five good opportunities to capture me. First, they might arrest me in the shopping district, which would be much quieter than the tourist quarter, with many more opportunities for the dreaded van to get in close. Second, they could snatch me from my hotel room while I slept. Third, they could pull my cab over on the highway to the airport. Fourth, they could box me in outside departures when the cab dropped me off. Fifth, they could ask the local equivalent of TSA to pull me out of the line for security and send me into secondary screening. This last option was the most likely, because it would be the cleanest. People get sent to secondary all the time, and for all kinds of reasons. Most come out the other side, but if one doesn't, who will notice? Until then, I would try my best to focus on the moment in hand: there was a lot to get through before I reached airport security, assuming I would get there at all.

After a while, the dark-blue car exited and was replaced, according to protocol, by the sharkskin sedan, which eventually also turned off. They probably replaced the gray car with yet another one in turn; but if so, I didn't see it.

At the shopping square, I headed for a menswear store I knew well. It was the Falcon equivalent of a Men's Wearhouse: large and utilitarian. Every inch of floor space was packed with shelves and racks displaying identical suits, shirts, and ties in conservative colors. I passed about forty minutes browsing, trying on a few things, and cultivating awareness of my surroundings. Aside from the omnipresent security cameras, I noticed no surveillance.

I decided to take this as a good sign. I ran a little calculation in my head. By now, it was early evening. As far as I knew, the same team had been following me since seven o'clock in the morning, going on twelve hours now. These were human beings, not supervillains: They would get tired. They would get hungry. They would have kids and significant others they wanted to see. At some point, they would clock off, and at that point they'd need to make the decision whether or not to call in a second shift to watch me in the evening and overnight. I wanted to make that answer an easy no. It was time to show the bear that I was winding down for the day. They could fall back on electronic surveillance until morning.

For the first time since I noticed my enhanced surveillance that morning, I returned to my hotel room. This time it felt different. If the Falconers had gone to the trouble of siccing a sophisticated team on me, they would for sure have bugged my room, too. It would be wired with, at the very least, a listening device and a camera. Most likely, the surveillance array would also include a thermal camera, so they could continue watching me even if I turned the lights off. As always, the important thing was not to be seen looking for these devices: I didn't want to offer the Falconers any further evidence that I was a trained spy. Just in case they were waiting until they had more dirt on me — more incriminating behavior than my eye contact with Bomberman in the arcade — before moving in for an arrest, I didn't want to do anything that would make their decision easier.

I picked up the crumpled paper that had been Jihi's origami lily. I ran my fingers over the words she had written inside. But now, instead of feeling comforted or aroused, I felt Jihi's absence weighing on me. Despite my heavy winter clothes, I was naked: alone and vulnerable behind enemy lines.

I told myself that if I wanted a fighting chance of seeing my wife again, I'd have to make it through the rest of the day. Put one foot in front of the other. Maintain what was left of my alias. It was the only hope I had.

Replacing my mahogany suit with athletic shorts and a cheap sweatshirt (the opposite of what Alex Hernandez—or indeed Andy Bustamante—would wear to a business meeting), I descended to the hotel restaurant for dinner, though I was far from hungry. Another aspect of the heightened state of awareness I had put myself in is that you don't taste anything: it's as if you shut off your senses of taste and smell in order to concentrate your energy on eyesight and hearing. I chewed and swallowed, but I was only going through the motions. Mainly, I was just showing my surveillance detail that I had no more meetings to go to. They could safely clock off.

Again I saw no surveillance, and again I decided to take that as a good sign. *They're turning in for the night,* I told myself.

Back in my room, I packed my suitcase and braced for the next period of peak risk. I knew that the SWAT team, if they were going to descend on me, wouldn't come too early: they wouldn't want to barge through crowds in the lobby. Nor would they come too late and risk waking guests up and causing a ruckus in the middle of the night. Based on this, I judged that prime time for a room invasion would be between 10 and 11 p.m. Late enough to be discreet, but early enough to be unsuspicious.

Around nine thirty, I switched on the TV, but kept it on mute. I sat on the bed, staring at the flickering image, listening. I put myself in a trancelike state, but not the kind that would take me to an imagined "happy place" or even a visualization of my future actions: if I didn't get through this moment, there would be no future to visualize. Instead, I practiced the kind of mindfulness meditation that promotes hypervigilance.

I heard every sound from the hallway outside. Hotel room doors opened and closed. Tourist couples chatted about their day's adventures. Drunk businesspeople celebrated deals well done. Sober ones headed for their beauty rest. After a while, the sounds tailed off. I braced for the knock on the door. The digital clock showed 22:59, then 23:00, then 23:01. The hour passed and they did not come for me. I felt my heart rate slow. My shoulders melted. I breathed.

With the immediate danger most likely passed, now it was time to get some rest. I took a hot shower to relax my muscles. I sat down again on the bed and wrote a note to myself in my journal in the form of a little shopping list, inspired by my trip to Falcon Men's Wearhouse: a coded aide-mémoire to help me remember the surveillance team and their vehicles.

"Gray shirt. White shirt. Blue shirt," I wrote. "Overcoat. Short jacket. Warm hat."

For my 5 a.m. wake-up, I set three separate alarms: my phone, my watch, and the hotel's clock radio. I also kept the blind on the window only three-quarters of the way down, so that if all else failed the sunlight might wake me up. But the real fail-safe was knowing that I would barely get any sleep at all. Occasionally, I did doze off for a few minutes. But I kept waking up again. At 2 a.m., a message came in from Acme that my flight had been changed. I was all set to leave on the 7:30 flight to Grizzly. As usual, the Kestrel-to-Grizzly leg of my trip would be on a Falcon-owned carrier, meaning that Falcon intelligence would know about my change of plans. They would have plenty of time to prepare their ambush.

Naturally, I rose before any of my three alarms went off. Outside my window, dawn struggled against the overcast skies. I wasn't hungry, but Alex Hernandez would be, so I forced myself down to the lobby to grab breakfast. Besides, I needed to show myself to whoever was following me now, to make damn sure they knew I was getting ready to leave: even at this late stage, surprising the tail would have been a fatal mistake, and appearing in the lobby unannounced with a packed suitcase would have risked doing exactly that.

I grabbed a hot coffee and a savory baked good from a little to-go table and took a final spin around the joint. It was a ghost town. No visible watchers. Which, given that this was a new day and they knew my travel plans, likely meant I was under the kind of surveillance you don't see. They would be able to track my cell phone all the way to Kestrel Airport.

My cab journey proved uneventful. I saw a couple of suspicious-looking vehicles on the highway, but I couldn't be sure that any of them were definitely following me: this route, from a popular hotel district to the main airport, was well traveled, after all. At departures, I paid the cabbie the outrageous fare he demanded and got out of the vehicle. I looked around for any rapidly approaching black panel vans, but again saw nothing.

That left the final bottleneck, and by far the most dangerous: secondary screening. Something like this exists in every country. Whenever passengers have to show a passport for entry or exit, there's always a minority who have issues with their visa status or whatever. To keep the flow going, the problem cases are taken out of the main line and sent to a separate room off to one side. Back there, it's secluded, quiet, and saturated with security personnel. People get sent to secondary for all sorts of reasons, most of them mundane. Nobody would notice if I didn't come out the other side. This would be their last opportunity to roll me up...but it would also be their best.

After checking in at the airline's one open desk, I approached the lane marked NON-FALCON EXIT. In front of it, space had been roped off for a long line, but it was still not yet 6 a.m. and there were just a handful of passengers waiting ahead of me. At the head of the line, a uniformed guard stood behind a portable podium with a laptop and a scanner. The guard swiped each passport and waved its owner through to security with a single repetitive motion. Scan, wave, pass. Scan, wave, pass. He looked half-asleep, which was exactly what I wanted.

I approached the podium and handed over Alex Hernandez's phony passport. The guard scanned it and waved me through. I took a half-step toward freedom. But then the guard's hand went up.

"Wait," he said. My heart stopped as he tapped on his laptop keyboard. He frowned at whatever message he was getting and tapped some more, as if trying to erase it. Finally, he sighed. "You changed your flight?"

"Yes. Actually, I finished my business here early, so..."

He shook his head. "Step out of the line. Okay. Go over there." He gestured to a little waiting area beside a keypad-locked door. "Someone will talk to you."

So this was it: I was about to enter secondary screening. In a daze, I made my way over to the waiting area. My mind traveled back again to my training. During the Major Bondoy debacle, the bad-cop interrogator screamed in my ear, poked me in the chest, practically spat in my face. That was mild. CIA would never deliberately cause its own people permanent injury, so there's no breaking of noses or tearing out of fingernails. But that didn't mean they couldn't inflict pain on us. Extreme cold, it turns out, is a pretty good substitute for the level of pain involved in torture. So the instructors would strip us naked and dunk us in ice water. They would shoot us with water hoses. They would disorient us by firing guns and exploding bombs nearby. Sometimes they would give us relatively mild electric shocks while burning a rabbit pelt to simulate the smell of our own flesh cooking. They were practiced enough to convince us that they had gone too far and were maiming us for real.

We were expected to endure all of this and more without surrendering a single secret. If you're captured, you never tell them what they want to hear. You are supposed to resist until you escape or they kill you.

"Alexander Hernandez?"

Two airport guards were standing over me. They were most likely in their late twenties, but in their ill-fitting uniforms they looked like two children playing dress-up. They escorted me through the keypad-locked door and down a narrow corridor. They walked fast and I lagged behind, negotiating the hallway with my rolling suitcase and satchel. Ahead of me, they turned into a side room, clearly expecting me to follow—but nevertheless letting the door slam shut in my face. This was odd, not because it was rude (in Falcon that's just how it is) but because you typically don't want to leave your captive alone. Theoretically, I could have bolted away down the corridor—that is, if I hadn't been savvy enough to realize how stupid an idea that would be in a secure zone of a secure building. Still, it was pretty unprofessional to leave me unsupervised on the other side of a closed door. Was this a test? Or was something else going on here?

Inside, the room was a cramped taupe box with blank walls. It smelled of Lysol. I tried not to think about what stains the bleach had removed. *This is the interrogation room,* my mind told me. *What will the holding cell look like? The jail? The prison?* The Falcon authorities didn't follow international norms for treatment of convicts. I'd heard of places where they gave you moldy bread to eat, intending for you to get sick, or where your meals would consist of a cup of water and a can of expired milk powder.

The young guards directed me to a plastic chair behind a metal folding table of the kind you might see in a marquee at an outdoor wedding. I had to shuffle a bit to get around the table with my suitcase and satchel.

I knew what would happen next. The two guards would leave and let me sit here for a half hour, maybe forty minutes. Long enough for me to get really rattled imagining the interrogation to follow. Then an interrogator from Falcon intelligence would make his entrance and the questioning would begin. I began steeling myself for it. I could use the silence of that forty-minute wait to prepare, mentally and physically. "Make the sweat box your prep box," as we say in training.

But then another odd thing happened. The two young guards pulled up two chairs and sat down opposite me. One opened up a laptop, while the other shuffled through a sheaf of papers.

"So," said Laptop. "You are Alexander Gustavo Hernandez, correct?"

*Wait,* I thought. *These guys are going to interrogate me themselves? And they're just going to launch right into it with no preamble? What's going on?*

"Why did you change your flight, Mister Hernandez?" said Laptop.

I told them the story I had settled on during lunch the previous day: I found the deal I was looking for on day one and was eager to get moving. I praised the quality of Falcon manufacturing, thinking this would go down well.

"I see. Were you perhaps unhappy in Falcon? Did you see something you didn't like?"

I was about to repeat my story when the other guard, Papers, chimed in.

"*Why* are you leaving?" he said, leaning forward for emphasis. "You can't leave. You should stay in Falcon. Stay like you planned!"

Laptop held up a hand and Papers fell silent. "Tell me about the people you met with," Laptop said. I told him about the two offices I had visited.

"Did you meet with anyone else?" I said I didn't.

"When were your appointments? Tell me how you got there. What did you do after your second meeting?" I gave him the answers, taking care to be as truthful and accurate as possible.

His questioning began to accelerate. He covered the same ground again, this time in more detail. How long exactly was the journey from the first meeting to the café? What was the name of my driver? What did I order at the café? Later, in the public square, why did I go to that restaurant? That bookstore? That arcade?

I began to think I had misjudged these guards. They might have looked like amateurs, but now they seemed to be using a classic counterintelligence ploy: asking detailed questions to which they already know the answers. In this way, you try to catch your target in a lie, no matter how small. Probe that tiny crack and you might just pry open their whole bullshit story. If they knew this much about my day yesterday, they must have had very detailed information on me. Sure, these guys might look young, they might behave less than professionally, they might have started the questioning right away instead of waiting. But all of these things could amount to a double bluff. Come to think of it, these guards might not be airport security at all — that would at least explain the ill-fitting uniforms. Was I already in the interrogation? Or were they just softening me up for the main event?

Laptop asked to go through my bags, and I was glad he did, because it gave me some respite from the questioning. I watched as Laptop and Papers turned everything over. My clothes. My two phones. My pocket litter in the name of Alex Hernandez. My journal with its shopping lists. My toiletry bag with a toothbrush and my retainers (I've had issues with my teeth all my life). I knew there would be nothing there to interest them.

They repacked my bags haphazardly and pushed them back toward me over the table. Then the questioning picked up again. They covered the same ground. I did my best to ensure that my answers remained exactly the same.

After we had been through my whole trip one more time, the questions slowed down. Now Laptop turned to his colleague and began barking questions at him instead. My Falconian wasn't good enough to understand much of what they were saying, but I did pick up Laptop using words like *when, why,* and *who.* Papers responded with variations on "I don't know" and "It doesn't make sense." Their conversation became a heated debate. It seemed Laptop had somewhere he would rather be, because he kept tapping his watch and gesturing to the door. Was he looking for the interrogator's silhouette in the frosted glass?

Finally, Laptop slammed shut the lid of his computer.

"We're done," he said. "You may go." Beside him, Papers looked dejected. But I didn't stick around to figure out why. I shuffled out from behind the table and followed the narrow corridor back into the terminal.

My flight to Grizzly was on the departure screens, marked BOARDING. I wanted to run with every fiber of my being, but even now, I had to avoid doing anything that might make me stand out. I made it to the gate with time to spare. The crowd of passengers moved toward the plane, excruciatingly slowly. I clutched Alex Hernandez's boarding pass and passport, still on guard for security to come and take me to the real interrogation.

Even once I was seated on the plane, I stayed tense, sweating into my pleather airline seat, ready for a heavy hand on my shoulder. I fixed my gaze on the door and kept a running tally in my head: every time someone came through who wasn't a police officer, I counted that as a point for me. After a few minutes, I saw a uniform. My blood ran cold, but it turned out to be the ground crew telling the flight attendants that everyone had boarded.

A flight attendant sealed the door: another point for me.

We pushed back from the stand: another point for me.

We taxied to the runway: another point for me.

With every point I won, I allowed myself to decompress a little more. But I knew that if the Falconers realized there was an American spy on the plane, they would have no hesitation in turning it around, so long as it was within their power to do so. Not until we entered Grizzly airspace did I dare even to think I was safe.

During my one-hour layover at Grizzly, I called Jihi and left a voicemail. "My love," I said, keeping my voice steady. "I'm in Grizzly. I'm feeling good. Everything worked out."

At the departure gate, there was nothing to eat but crummy fast food. It didn't matter. I practically inhaled my meal, and it was the best thing I ever tasted.

The other shoe had dropped. But it wasn't a jackboot. It was a slipper.

## JIHI

I checked my watch for the four hundredth time that afternoon. By the time I heard Andy's voicemail at lunch, his connecting flight was already in the air. Would he have landed in Wolf by now? Was he on his way back to the office? My thoughts bounced off the walls. For hours, I had roamed the building, looking for people to talk to about anything and everything: work, weekend plans, their kids, anything. After a while, I told myself to sit down. I might as well get some work done. I sat down at my desk and stared at my latest database search results, still too excited to do anything meaningful.

Around dinnertime, I heard the door to my office open. Andy came in smiling and planted a kiss on my forehead. We had an unspoken rule that in the office we'd keep public displays of affection to a minimum. Just this once, I broke it. I jumped up and gave Andy a big hug around his shoulders.

"Oh my God, I was so..." I was about to say *worried,* but I checked myself. You never knew which colleagues might be listening, and there was no sense in freaking anybody out. So I just said, "I'm glad you're home." The tearful reunion would have to wait.

## ANDY

Kissing Jihi was the first thing on my mind, but it wasn't the first thing I did after I arrived back at the Wolf office. Operational protocol dictated that I put the doomed Alex Hernandez character to bed by depositing his documents back in the security box and replacing them with my own. Besides, I would feel a lot more like myself once I got that wedding ring back on my finger.

Like Jihi, I was working hard to contain my emotions. I still wasn't sure what had just happened to me, and I definitely didn't want anyone else leaping to conclusions, especially since Tasha had only just started working inside Falcon and we expected Luke and Beverly would begin to do the same in due course. I didn't want to freak any of them out.

While Jihi went out to get dinner for us, I went to James's office and threw the burner phone down on his desk, with the charms from the knockoff store attached.

"Say," he said. "Wasn't this thing supposed to be stashed under a bridge somewhere?"

"Well, now it's on your desk, buddy. Happy birthday. Hope you like sparkly charms."

Jihi came in with takeout and James fetched us each a beer. I gave them the play-by-play of my trip: the lack of bumbling minders; the vehicle and pedestrian surveillants; the close encounters at the restaurant, the bookstore, and the arcade; the arrest that never came; the weird-ass interrogation at the airport.

"Oh man," said James. "You got lucky."

"Excuse me?"

"Yeah, dude." James laid out his theory, based on his vastly superior knowledge of Falcon intelligence and of Falcon in general.

It started at the arcade. If Bomberman had reported making eye contact with me, his supervisors would have known I was aware of the team following me. I would have been arrested on the spot, no questions asked. But Bomberman had made a mistake: by making eye contact with me, he revealed himself to me just as much as I exposed myself to him. And if there's one thing Falcon intelligence will not tolerate, it's mistakes. Bomberman was not about to risk his career and his family's livelihood just to capture some punk American. It was a classic cover-your-ass move of the kind that happens in bureaucracies the world over. But this time, that ass-covering impulse saved my life.

Absent the crucial report from Bomberman, the Falconers still didn't know for sure I was a spy. They would have planned to keep tailing me the following day, hoping to catch me meeting a source or otherwise conducting espionage. As on day two, they would presumably have aimed to pick me up as I was leaving the hotel, no earlier than around 7:30 a.m. Overnight, as I had hoped, they had fallen back on passive digital surveillance. Without confirmation that I was an intelligence officer, my case would not warrant a night shift.

With nobody watching my activities in real time, they didn't notice that I had changed my flight until the guard at the non-Falcon exit line scanned Alex Hernandez's passport at ten to six the next morning. At that point, over at Falcon intelligence HQ, some poor duty officer's computer must have lit up like a Christmas tree.

James thought that Falcon intelligence probably asked border security to keep me there as long as possible while they scrambled an interrogator from headquarters. Papers got the call, but he knew his English wasn't up to the job, so he roped in the nearest fluent speaker: Laptop. When I heard Laptop using the words *who, why,* and *when,* he was most likely asking Papers, "*Who* the hell says we have to keep this guy?" and "*Why* are we doing this?" and "*When's* it going to be done?" Laptop had other shit to do, and he wasn't going to get a promotion by holding some American businessman who had a flight to catch. As for Papers, he was piggy in the middle. All he could say was "I don't know." And neither of them sought clarification from the higher-ups, because that would mean admitting that they didn't know what was going on and laying themselves bare to the kind of draconian punishment Falcon metes out to incompetents.

Meanwhile, few staff at Falcon intelligence would have been clamoring to take on a brand-new counterintelligence case at 6 a.m., with the strong risk of making an error of their own. Eventually, the system just reverted to the mean: it did nothing.

James grinned. "If you'd been there at prime time, with your surveillance buddies on duty? Oh, man. You'd still be there now."

I wished I could have taken credit for my escape. But I saw the truth in James's explanation: Falcon bureaucracy had stymied itself. The system's notorious ruthlessness had turned out to be both its strength and its undoing: when things went right, it was unstoppable; but when they went wrong, even a little bit, all the cogs in the machine seized up. Everyone focused on protecting themselves, rather than doing the job at hand.

For a moment, we enjoyed the image of the Falconers scrambling to clean up the mess I had left behind. The schadenfreude was delicious. Then Jihi asked the million-dollar question.

"What do we think this means for our cell?"

We didn't know for sure, of course. But most likely, it was the Falcon mole—the very person that our cell had been set up to thwart—who had unmasked me to their handlers. After all, I was the only point of contact between the Cell and Falcon House, and thus the only team member who would have been visible to the mole. Assuming that I was a case officer in the traditional sense, Falcon intelligence had sent a surveillance team to see who I was meeting. The team must have been mighty confused when the answer turned out to be: two medium-size companies.

So Falcon had found our trip wire—me—and was tugging on it. Thanks to the cell model, I hadn't led them to any of our contacts, because I was not directly working those contacts. But what about the other members of the Cell? Were they now exposed, too?

Again, we couldn't know for sure. But none of our other teammates reported any additional security, inside Falcon or outside. All indications were that they had gone undetected—that their covers, unlike mine, had remained intact, just as the cell model was designed to ensure.

Of course, this still left many other questions unanswered. Why, for instance, had Bridge attracted a minder? Why had Kingpin, Converse, and other Falcon contacts around the world become harder to meet with? Why had traveling Falconers been ordered to work with Wander instead of non-Falcon fixers? Had Falcon caught onto our activities through other counterintelligence means, as well as through their mole?

The most likely answer was none of the above: the Falconers simply tightened security across the board, not just for our targets but for anyone dealing with foreigners. There was only one reason to impose such a blanket policy: they couldn't do anything more targeted, because they didn't know whom to target. Their mole, blind to the rest of our cell, couldn't give them anything beyond a single name: Alex Hernandez. Our cell model was working. We were beating the mole.

"Well," said James, "I guess I'll leave you to it. You've got a shit-ton of work to do. Sorry, Jihi."

"Don't apologize to me," Jihi said. "I'm heading home for a hot bath. It's Andy who's going to be here all night."

"Jesus," I said. "Thanks for the pep talk."

As annoying as it was, they were right. I had come through hell to get back here. All I wanted to do was take a shower (preferably with Jihi) and collapse into bed. But I couldn't do that. In fact, it was far from the end of my workday. Now that I was back in a secure environment, it was time to write my reports—and given the events of the past thirty-six hours, there was a lot to report.

If Hollywood is ever brave or dumb enough to make a truly accurate spy movie, a good 80 percent of its run time will consist of the spy sitting in front of a computer, typing reports. Intelligence is about information, but it's no good just collecting the information: you have to ensure that it gets to the right people, at the right time, in the right format. Even for a government job, the amount of paperwork is truly exorbitant.

What is more, a report of high-level surveillance on a CIA officer in the Falcon capital was bound to attract immediate attention from all sorts of people at Langley. I knew that as soon as I filed my report, my secure email and chat would light up like a Christmas tree with urgent messages seeking more detail. Jihi was right, as usual: this was going to be an all-nighter.

# PART XI
# THE RECKONING

## JIHI

Following Andy's narrow escape from Falcon, one thought haunted us above all: could his unmasking have stemmed not from the mole but from a mistake we made ourselves?

We knew that Langley would soon be crawling all over our operations with a view to answering exactly that question. If the Cell was to survive at all, we would need to get out ahead of them with an investigation of our own.

James, Andy, and I spent a week scouring everything we had ever done as a unit, looking for any indication we might have put a foot wrong. James grilled Andy on exactly what he saw in Kestrel. What make and model was each vehicle? How many minutes did they have someone behind you? How many turns did that equate to? How many glances did you get at each surveillant? Can you nail their ages to within plus or minus three years and their heights to within plus or minus three inches? And on and on.

Meanwhile, I looked at our operations as a whole. From tracking Converse, I knew how damaging it could be when the data connected two people who shouldn't be connected. Had we made that mistake? Had we inadvertently linked Cell members to each other, maybe on social media or in conversation with our sources? Had somebody let slip one of our true names? I combed our records and interviewed every member of the Cell, applying in reverse the same techniques we knew Falcon intelligence would have used against us.

But from what we could tell, our record was spotless, and we reported as much to Langley. We knew their response would take a couple of weeks. Ordinarily, Andy and I would have taken the opportunity to travel. But Andy didn't want to get on a plane again so soon after his ordeal, so we enjoyed a Wolfian staycation.

As we strolled the streets, casually window-shopping, I squeezed Andy's hand and brought him in close. "You almost lost all this. We almost lost you."

"You're right," he said, his face grave. "I hadn't thought about it that way." Then he smiled his familiar grin. "Hey, doesn't it look like that mannequin is taking a dump?"

## ANDY

I wasn't ready to confront what had happened to me in Kestrel—let alone what could have happened. To be honest, once I was done with the intensive debriefs that I had to endure for work, I couldn't bring myself to think about those days in any detail until we started preparing to write this book.

In the weeks that followed my escape from Falcon, CIA repeatedly offered me counseling—standard procedure for an officer who went through this kind of trauma. Jihi encouraged me to take up the offer, pointing out that CIA had helped her through her anxiety right at the start, and it hadn't stopped her becoming a superstar in her field. But I turned it down. Among field operators, there was a stigma around any kind of mental health treatment. Frankly, it stemmed from an unhealthy macho impulse: "I don't need anyone to help me feel better!" I don't know if that culture has changed by now, but for everyone's sake, it really should.

Even as I scorned psychological treatment, I noticed a subtle but permanent shift in my personality. Whereas before I was always charging toward the next objective, now I found myself more inclined to enjoy the moment. The smell of fresh coffee. The atmosphere of a city. Later, the feeling of holding my children in my arms. In short, I think I grew up a little. And it started in Wolf with the overwhelming sense of peace and contentment I felt amid the winking lights and window displays and shitting mannequins.

At the same time, we knew that in just a couple of weeks, we would reap the whirlwind. Our consciences were clear: thanks to the scrub we had carried out, we believed with high confidence that our operations were not the source of my unmasking. But in the end, that might not matter. Langley could still use the incident in Kestrel as an excuse to shut us down. We had suspected from the very beginning that we were being set up to fail, and with a mole hunt still active, Falcon House was even more suspicious of outsiders than usual. It would be so easy to declare the Cell a failed experiment and revert to the old ways—even when those old ways had gotten the Agency into this mess in the first place.

Sure enough, a few weeks later a team of three investigators arrived from Falcon House's counterintelligence division. We braced ourselves for a full-scale witch hunt, complete with lie-detector tests and shouted accusations, but it wasn't like that at all. The team did interview each member of the Cell (including Will, our tech guru, and Dianna, our linguist) one-on-one, but their questions were more pro forma than probing. Our own scrub had already gone into much more detail. In fact, the investigators seemed unaware of key pieces of information: the fact that Luke and Beverly were both working on different sources at the same time, for example, or the role Tasha's family played in her relationship with Kingpin.

What did this slipshod approach mean? I was convinced that it spelled doom for the Cell. Langley already knew they were going to pull the plug, so they felt there was no need for a real investigation. Having wrapped up their inquiries, the team returned to headquarters. We waited for word that we were getting shut down. But the fallout never came.

At the time, this was puzzling. But later we found out why we were spared. Annika, the spike-heeled No. 3, had gone to bat for us. She had made it clear to Falcon House that the Cell was delivering results; that she trusted the outcome of our internal scrub; and most important of all, that she would not tolerate on her turf anything that might distract us at this critical juncture.

Having been so dismissive of our efforts in the beginning, now Annika was staking her reputation on protecting the Cell from those in Falcon House counterintelligence who might otherwise have sought to close it down. Without top cover from a case officer of her caliber, we might have been toast. As was typical of Annika, she never breathed a word of it to us.

## JIHI

By the fourth quarter of that year, there was no denying it: the Cell was delivering the goods. The Falcon policy on talking to Americans hadn't changed; in fact, if anything it had gotten more restrictive. But our case officers were just so good that they found ways to get their sources talking regardless. They made themselves so valuable, so interesting, so compelling, so seemingly innocent that our targets couldn't see why there would be a problem being friends with them—and opening up to them.

For instance, James successfully used Bridge's discontent with the increased surveillance on him to pull the engineer closer than ever. Now, based on Bridge's grumbling and name-dropping, James was cultivating a network of people inside Falcon: engineers, scientists, project managers. The kind of people who would know which government programs were getting funded. James kept them talking by displaying so much enthusiasm about their specialties in science, technology, and innovation that they couldn't resist chatting to a fellow nerd. On a more mercenary level, James held out the possibility (explicit or implied) that he might someday be able to get these folks jobs in the West, where, unlike in Falcon, innovation is rewarded and talented individuals are recognized for their achievements.

Luke was a regular at the bathhouse favored by Zefram, our super-connected white whale in Wolf. We all enjoyed the image of Luke sitting nude and chatting to similarly naked, droopy old men. In time, Luke even bumped Zefram, striking up a conversation in which they exchanged pleasantries for about five minutes. Despite Luke's obviously being an American, Zefram didn't give him the cold shoulder. Slowly, subtly, Luke began laying the foundations for a friendship. Meanwhile, officers elsewhere had begun to cultivate relationships with staff at the leading glioma clinics in Western Europe, preparing the ground for the day when Luke steered the conversation around to Zefram Jr.'s treatable eye condition.

Tasha got back onto Kingpin's calendar with her usual jiu-jitsu, turning her weaknesses—young, female, American—into strengths. She kept up her relationship with Mrs. Kingpin on the basis that

Monty and Kingpin Jr. missed each other. Gradually, Kingpin himself drifted back into the picture. With a security crackdown underway, he appreciated a confidante he could speak to without fear that she would report him to the Falcon authorities. Besides, what was the harm in speaking to someone as innocent as young, hippie Tasha? She was an open book, wasn't she?

Based on the information Tasha reported, I was able to identify even more valuable contacts for her within Kingpin's network: potential sources involved in, for example, finding sites for new military bases and building secure telecommunications infrastructure. These were people with high-level, sensitive access—exactly the kind of people America needed to be talking to—and Tasha reached them via a node, Kingpin, whom she had cultivated through a family friendship. Were it not for the cell model, we might never have gotten to these juicy sources at all: Tasha might still be wasting her time with Justice, the long-winded stone merchant she met on the conference circuit.

The folks Tasha spoke to were slick managerial types who had relationships to maintain with Falcon officials. This meant they were more suspicious of foreigners than the nerds James was cultivating, but businesspeople still need to make money, and in the global economy you don't do that by staying home. True to form, Tasha pressed her advantage. From Kingpin's information, for example, we were able to figure out which government projects would need to procure stuff from the West—a particular type of engine made only in Europe, let's say. Tasha could swoop in at just the right moment with an offer to broker a purchase of exactly what they needed.

To our delight, Tasha's success attracted attention from the higher-ups at Langley, and Falcon House was in the process of bringing her in as one of their own: quite the coup for a flower child who didn't speak Falconian. Tasha's advancement was a point of special pride for us, because it showed that our cell model didn't just deliver intelligence: it functioned as a showcase for talents like Tasha who otherwise might have gotten overlooked. We lost track of Tasha after she was absorbed into Falcon House. But we strongly suspected that she was flying high in service of the United States.

The best news of all, at least from an intelligence-gathering point of view, came from Beverly's courtship of Converse, the young intelligence officer stationed in Wolf. Beverly played the friend card and it worked. Converse, it turned out, did still want to meet up, she just wanted to do so in more private settings. For example, instead of a regular table at a restaurant, she wanted a private room. But she was willing to let Beverly continue to pick the times and venues. To a case officer, this is the dream scenario: instead of running scared when the new Falcon security policy came in, Converse was asking for greater confidentiality, and she was trusting Beverly to make that happen. When that happens, it represents a big step along the road to making your contact a formal, witting intelligence source. In other words, Beverly was on course toward creating an American mole inside Falcon intelligence.

## ANDY

The Cell survived and thrived. What was the logical next step? A whole network of cells, operating autonomously but linked up through isolated points of contact. That was the real strength of the bin Laden–inspired model we were forging: the ability to turn individual groups of actors into a resilient and devastatingly effective network. For a terrorist group, of course, the end goal was to sow chaos in furtherance of their extremist ideologies. For us, the aim was to defend and strengthen the United States in furtherance of democratic values. And for that to happen, our fellow spooks needed our help to get their own cells up and running.

So we decided to spread the gospel of the Cell. We convened an international conference in Wolf, inviting around a dozen officers from the Intelligence Community worldwide, all of whom were cultivating Falcon sources of their own.

Being so open about our activities, even within the Agency, was a security risk for us. Anyone we invited to the conference might theoretically have been in touch with the mole. Hell, they could have *been* the mole. But we judged that it was a risk worth taking. The Cell was succeeding where old-school methods had failed. Imagine what we could achieve with a whole network of cells. Intelligence agencies typically distribute information on a need-to-know basis. If we wanted to bring the cell model to full effectiveness, these other teams needed to know.

Getting everyone to Wolf took some logistical acrobatics: we knew from our experience with Converse how dangerous a slipup in arrangements could be. We had to give each of them a different itinerary and cover for action.

The conference lasted several days. I kicked it off with a welcome presentation about the virtues of the cell model. Our conferees arrived knowing very little about how the model worked. Partly this was deliberate, out of the need for secrecy. But mostly it was because the attendees only read the invitation as far as "Location: Wolf." Wolf is always a fun place to be, and it's an especially welcome respite if you happen to be stationed in a difficult or dangerous spot.

"There's nothing revolutionary about what we're doing here," I told the conference. Around the room, people were scribbling copious notes. "We're just marrying two successful approaches. One is Intelligence Community best practice. The other is terrorism."

A dozen pens stopped dead. A dozen pairs of eyes swiveled to meet mine, eyebrows raised. Maybe I could have eased into that one a little more gracefully.

I cleared my throat. "So, uh, now that I have your attention..."

James gave a talk on the nuances of Falcon culture that we had been able to exploit. Jihi pinned up a spider diagram of the networks derived from Bridge, Kingpin, and Wander, showing the substantial overlap between them. The targeters in the room nodded with appreciation for a job so expertly done. As for the case officers, their jaws hit the floor, just as we saw happen when Jihi first flexed her targeting muscles for the Cell team. During the break, they bum-rushed Jihi, asking how they could get Langley to assign them a targeter of their own.

The next day consisted of workshops in which we imagined how the cell model could be applied to real-life cases the attendees were working on (anonymized and obfuscated for security). At least two of our guests had sources whom they were under pressure to dump on the basis that they'd already squeezed all the intelligence out of them—the same criticism James had faced over Bridge. As the day went on, you could see them getting more and more excited about the possibilities.

In the end, however, the results of the conference proved mixed. For intelligence officers trained in the traditional ways, it was a tough idea to get their heads around—let alone sell to their local equivalents of Annika. Ultimately, most of our conferees took a pass on the cell model: only a few decided to adopt it.

That was how I assumed it would pan out. The cell model would survive—Langley had allowed it to do so—but it would remain a minority idea that only a handful of weirdos would be into. It would never catch on in a big way. Or so I thought.

## JIHI

With all our contacts bearing fruit, and more on the way, and with Andy out there spreading the word, the Cell was busier than ever. But I found myself feeling increasingly sluggish, which in turn made it difficult to concentrate on my work at a critical moment. After ruling out a few other possibilities, I zeroed in on the culprit: I had an ovarian cyst while in Wolf and was prescribed a three-month course of birth-control pills. Fatigue was among the side effects. When the three months were up, I breathed a sigh of relief and went back to using the rhythm method for contraception, little knowing that the pills had knocked my cycle out by a week.

A predictable result ensued, and pretty soon, instead of worrying about being captured by Falcon intelligence, I was dealing with morning sickness and mood swings. Ironically, it was my focus on my career that led to our starting a family. We wondered: as parents, would we feel differently about intelligence work? That would turn out to be a prescient question.

Our two-year tour was almost up. Everyone assumed we would be extended. Annika gave me a glowing review and even got me an award for exceptional performance (neither of which, true to form, she ever mentioned to me). She and the rest of the Wolf leadership made clear that they wanted to retain us. We were excited to see how the Cell would develop.

But Langley had other plans for me and Andy. Both of us were recalled to headquarters, with immediate effect, and promoted into more senior roles within Falcon House.

We chafed against this decision. We created the Cell together. Wouldn't we be more useful here in the field, running it? Annika went to bat for us again, but this time Langley insisted.

As it turned out, we were victims of our own success. We knew our model worked, but we assumed that expanding it would have to be a grassroots effort, and that the higher-ups would be the hardest ones to convince. In reality, it was the other way around: Langley got it, even if a lot of people further down the hierarchy didn't. Now headquarters wanted us to train a new batch of cells, to be deployed against Falcon targets all over the world. It turned out that we didn't need to hold a conference in order to spread the gospel of the cell model. The results spoke for themselves. We comforted ourselves with the thought that, from Langley, we could potentially sow the seeds for dozens more groups just like the one we built in Wolf.

Leaving Wolf was bittersweet for personal reasons as well as professional ones. The cell model relied on utmost secrecy, with minimal contact between the cell and the outside world, and we had no intention of making hypocrites of ourselves. That meant we had to sever all contact with our colleagues: James, Dianna, Will, Tasha, Beverly, and Luke. That's how it has been to this day. We hope that one day, maybe when they are retired or otherwise leave the service, they will feel ready to reach out. As of this writing, that day has not come.

## SCIMITAR

Scimitar submitted his application to rejoin the Intelligence Community. Was this a sudden change of heart? Had his first encounter with the private sector made Scimitar a patriot again? Had he decided to devote his life to government service after all—poor pay and lack of recognition notwithstanding? Unlikely. If anything, his resentment toward CIA would only have grown. Most probably, he already knew his next move. By cozying up to the Agency once more, he was trying to maximize his potential value as a Falcon asset. It wasn't unheard-of for the tortuous vetting processes to take years, but evidently his Falcon handlers weren't satisfied with his progress because Scimitar received a needling email from them. The subject line this time referred by name to John and Jacob, Scimitar's twin sons. Apparently, Falcon intelligence knew very well why Scimitar felt he needed their dirty money.

"How are the boys?" the handler wrote. "Doing well in school? We haven't seen them for a while. Maybe they've decided not to go to college after all." The translation was obvious: make yourself useful again or face the consequences.

No doubt Falcon intelligence was frustrated at Scimitar's lack of progress. But it was not for want of trying on Scimitar's part. He went through the usual multiple rounds of interviews to rejoin the Intelligence Community. His prospects must have seemed good, because he even moved his family back to the US, and they settled in the Maryland suburbs of Washington, DC.

Unfortunately for Scimitar—but fortunately for the Cell and the United States—it was a setup. The feds were using fake interviews to get Scimitar on record telling lies—about his trips to Falcon, about the solvency of the company he set up with the former official, about his continued possession of classified materials. Meanwhile, the FBI—which has responsibility for investigating moles on US soil—was closing in. During his stays in Maryland and in his hometown in the Midwest, the feds searched his belongings and found classified information. Scimitar tried to hide the folders, but the feds were able to find them.

As a trained operator, Scimitar must have known that the classified information was not secure in his possession. So it is worth asking: why was Scimitar traveling with all those documents? In short, he had to guard his stock-in-trade. Falcon intelligence knew he was gathering this information. Instead of paying him for it, why not break into his house overseas and take it for free? It wasn't as if Scimitar could call the police to report the theft. To avoid jeopardizing the source of his lavish income, Scimitar likely decided to take his chances and carry the documents with him wherever he went, betting that the Americans didn't know about his treason. He was wrong.

Scimitar felt the noose tightening and fled the country. It seems the FBI let him go. We don't know why. Maybe they wanted more evidence against him. Maybe they hoped that he would lead them to his handlers. Maybe they simply lost track of him.

One thing is clear: Scimitar's usefulness to Falcon intelligence was spent. Within six months, his payments from his handlers — said to have totaled in the hundreds of thousands — had dried up completely. A couple of years later, he was working as a car salesman: quite the comedown for a man who was once an invaluable Falcon asset with dozens of lives in the palm of his hand. But Scimitar had not yet reached his lowest ebb.

# PART XII
# A WHOLE NEW MOUSETRAP

## ANDY

When I read the *Washington Post* that morning, I nearly spat out my cornflakes.

> CIA Director John Brennan is considering sweeping organizational changes that could include breaking up the separate spying and analysis divisions that have been in place for decades to create hybrid units focused on individual regions and threats to US security.

In other words, Brennan was proposing to make the cell model, with its small teams and mixed skill sets, the modus operandi for the whole damn Agency.

"My love!" I yelled to Jihi, jabbing a finger at the article. "Look what they're doing with your idea!"

Maybe the wholesale adoption of the cell model shouldn't have come as much of a surprise. When we arrived in Wolf, we found a human intelligence network with literally zero productive sources. When we left, just two years later, Bridge was gushing like a firehose; the team had created several more leads from scratch; we had a Falcon intelligence officer well on the way to formal asset status; we were closing in on our white whale, Zefram; and in case any of those didn't work out, Jihi had built up dossiers on more than a dozen additional targets. Plus, we had begun training cells in other parts of the world to use our methods to collect intelligence from Falcon sources in third-country locations around the world. We weren't allowed to know the outcomes of their cases — the cell model depended on secrecy, after all — but for the model to be adopted Agency-wide, they must have enjoyed tremendous success.

By the time of the *Washington Post* write-up, however, we had left CIA.

Proud as we were of our service and the Cell's achievements, as newly minted middle managers we soon became painfully aware that office politics were as rife at CIA as in any other workplace. And for some of our bosses, loyalty and hierarchy seemed to matter more than merit.

It took a long time to replace Jihi at the Wolf office, because two feuding managers kept rejecting each other's choices. Finally, they painted themselves into a corner and wound up appointing a mediocre targeter whose only qualification was being favored by neither side. This person had a reputation for talking more than they worked: always bragging about their abilities without doing anything to justify the boast. They went to Wolf and immediately started trying to order the case officers about, which at CIA never goes down well. Talk about being promoted to your level of incompetence. We don't know for sure what the outcome was, of course, but given how pivotal Jihi's role was, the Cell must have suffered as a result.

I had a similarly mind-boggling experience while working to facilitate an airdrop of hardware to an active operation in a war zone (I can't say which one). By this time, I had been promoted again and been transferred from Falcon House to a different division. The operation I was working on required a funds transfer within a couple of hours or it would fail. The two managers above me were unavailable, so I approved the money myself. The op went off, and everyone agreed that the swift transfer was crucial to the mission's success.

But instead of a commendation, I received a reprimand. My boss's boss, furious at being left out of the loop, subjected me to a tirade about my "loyalty," which of course he felt I owed not to the mission but to him. It was like being back in the Air Force: once again, the system was trying to mold me into a blind rule-follower—or worse, a political game-player.

## JIHI

With the mole hunt still in full swing, the atmosphere at Langley was tense. The whispering, always a feature of Falcon House, was worse than ever. Occasionally it would bubble over into outright finger-pointing. A few months before Andy and I got out, a good friend of ours decided it was time for her to leave CIA. This was somebody I knew well. We trained together and subsequently worked together when I was assigned against Badger. Her marriage broke down, and while she was on assignment in the same region as Falcon, she met someone new. Falcon House wanted to rotate her out of there, but she wanted to stay with her new man (the fact that he was a hot martial-arts instructor probably factored into her decision). The only way to do that was to quit the Agency. She lined up a job with a big US-based consulting firm.

Her departure kicked up a hornet's nest of rumor and accusations. People were whispering that she was the mole all along, and that by leaving she was getting away with it. Knowing the full story, I tried to defend our friend's reputation as best I could, but the allegations continued to fly.

It was dismaying to see all of this. Instead of our being united against a common threat, it seemed as if the mole succeeded in making CIA officers snipe at each other. By behaving this way, we were playing directly into the hands of Falcon intelligence. At the same time, Andy and I were reminded that leaving, though painful, was at least possible.

I asked another friend for advice on engineering our exit. In particular, I wanted to know what he thought would be appropriate to put on our résumés. Contrary to popular belief, former CIA officers aren't required to keep silent forever about having worked there—but it's definitely the case that when you leave CIA, you can't write a detailed résumé right away. Our friend was somebody Andy and I had met on our first day of orientation at the Agency. He was adorably proud to work for CIA, which had been his ambition since he was a kid. After training, he became a counterintelligence officer, a job that requires a great deal of caution. I sought his counsel on the résumé question precisely because he was so security-conscious and I valued his views.

He gave me friendly advice, essentially telling me to make my own assessment of the likely risks and use my best judgment. But afterward, I was shocked to find out that he had sent out a blast email to everyone we had ever trained with or worked with. *Do not trust the Bustamantes,* his message said. *They are a risk to the Agency. If they try to contact you, ignore them. Report the matter to me immediately.*

After we made so much progress to defeat the mole, being accused in this way—especially by someone we knew and trusted—came as a slap in the face. Ultimately, though, Andy and I learned how to live with suspicion, bad management, even low salaries. The deciding factor in our leaving the Agency was something else entirely.

As we suspected while I was pregnant in Wolf, having a baby wound up transforming our outlook on pretty much everything. Jet-setting around the world, chasing bad guys, dodging foreign intelligence—when you are young and free, these things seem daring and exciting and sexy. But later, when a little life depends on you, it all starts to look very different.

We kept coming back to one of the imprisoned case officers we learned about in training. On the day of his arrest, his daughter was two years old. By the time he was released, she was in her twenties and her father was a stranger to her. He never saw her grow up. The girl was robbed of a father. And for what? A medal for valor and his back pay. No trophy, no amount of money, not even the satisfaction of having served honorably and faithfully, could compensate for a loss like the one that case officer and his family suffered.

Leaving aside the risk of capture or death, we heard of way too many officers whose families were strained or even blown apart by years of keeping secrets from one another. When is the time ever right to tell your kids that mommy and daddy have been lying to them their whole lives? In practice, it's left up to individual officers to use their best judgment. We heard about one senior manager who decided to tell his twin children when they were thirteen years old. One of the twins thought dad's job was pretty cool, but the other one started spouting conspiracy theories about how CIA was supposedly involved in drugs and human trafficking. Now his family was at war with itself—not to mention the risk posed to his career by a disgruntled teenager and self-styled whistleblower.

On a practical level, the leadership track meant long hours and little outside time. As we rose (or more accurately, were forced) up through CIA's ranks, we found ourselves struggling to make time to spend with our son—or, for that matter, to afford child care on our mediocre government salaries. Increasingly, our existing role as intelligence officers seemed incompatible with our new role as parents.

At last, we reached a pivotal realization. We were prepared to die for our country, but we were not prepared to destroy our family. After seven years of service, we decided to quit CIA.

Not that they made it easy on the way out. CIA security sat us down in a windowless room and grilled us for hours on our contacts with foreign nationals (minimal), income we had outside of work (none), or any outside business interests (you must be joking). Then came a stern lecture about our lifetime duty to protect classified information, followed by dire threats of federal jail time should we breach those obligations. They scowled at us the whole time, like bad cops bullying a confession out of a suspect. They might as well have whipped out the lie-detector: facing those security officers was like being hooked up to a human polygraph.

And as soon as we were out the door, life on the outside smacked us in the face. With what looked like a seven-year gap in both of our work histories, we struggled to find any employer interested in hiring us. Lacking better options, we moved to my parents' house in Florida. Or, more specifically, their garage. After the glamor of the Cell and Falcon House, this new reality was a bitter pill to swallow. Ultimately, though, leaving the Agency was the only possible decision for our growing family. In our service to the United States, we felt we had made the contribution of a lifetime with the development of the cell model. Now our children needed us. We owed them a debt of service, too.

# EPILOGUE

After a slow start to life on the outside, we made our way to corporate America, where we spent five years as executives, using our spy skills to build relationships, win negotiations, and secure career advancement. What we really craved, though, was the freedom of running our own business. Working for CIA had transformed our lives; what if we could give ordinary folks a taste of that magic?

So we finally took the plunge. To prove our concept, we developed an experience called "One Day as a Spy" and invited potential investors to take part. Participants spent the morning learning core spy skills: dead drops, bumps, asset meetings. In the afternoon, participants would go out and apply those skills in a simulated operation in a major US city. It was just like the sim with Major Bondoy on the Farm, except this time nobody got arrested (we weren't that mean).

The investors loved it, the funding flowed in, and a business was born. We called our company EverydaySpy, because we believe that spycraft can be useful in all kinds of situations—but that's a story for another book.

*　*　*

Years later, for reasons we can only guess at, Scimitar decided that the coast was clear for him to return to the United States once again. The FBI had other ideas. Federal agents arrested him in the arrivals hall at O'Hare.

When we first heard the news about Scimitar's arrest and the charges filed against him, we had a flood of conflicting emotions. Relief that justice was being served, of course. But also shock at seeing the face of the traitor we had worked so hard against. Questions we never dared to ask ourselves in the past now crept into our conversations: Was it he that turned Andy's name over to Falcon intelligence? How close did he get to finding Jihi? How much information did he really give to Falcon? How long would it take for the US to build back after the damage he caused? Was he the only mole we were working against?

The indictment against Scimitar charged him only with "conspiracy to gather or deliver national defense information to aid a foreign government" and "unlawful retention of national defense information." He took a plea deal and was convicted on a single charge.

We understand why Scimitar was not charged with espionage or treason. Those crimes are hard to prove, and rightly so, since they potentially carry the death penalty. Unlike in Falcon and many other places, a conviction requires evidence, and CIA will only adduce information it's prepared to declassify. Besides, by charging a US citizen with a rap sheet of lurid offenses, you telegraph to the American people that they aren't safe. To be sure, it was galling to see Scimitar charged only with comparatively minor offenses, given the potentially shattering consequences of his betrayal. But perhaps in silent recognition of those consequences, his sentence was heavy. Assuming he serves the full stretch, by the time he is released he will be a very old man.

So much for our mole. Or, at least, for one of them. In a society like the United States, where people's privacy is protected by law, and freedom is valued as highly as security, there will always be turncoats who choose to exploit our country's openness in exchange for their own personal gain. Around the same time as Scimitar, we know that Falcon intelligence was running other moles inside the US government, and not just at CIA. It goes without saying that these are just the moles we know about, and that Falcon is only one of America's geopolitical adversaries. At any given moment, the counterintelligence threats against the United States are dizzying to contemplate, and the risks monumental.

Nevertheless, given the choice, we know for a fact that almost every American would gladly accept these risks instead of the alternative: turning our country into a surveillance society. As the saying goes, the price of liberty is eternal vigilance. The challenge, then, is to stay ahead of the moles. And in that respect, the best defense is a good offense— which is where, we hope, the model we helped to establish will continue to pay dividends for our country long into the future.

# APPENDIX

To protect current CIA tradecraft tools and methods, operational tradecraft described in this memoir represents techniques from across the US Intelligence Community and should not be attributed to CIA directly. Explore the links below to learn more about the tradecraft exemplified in this book.

## EVERYDAYSPY
**www.everydayspy.com/shadowcell**
Visit this link for a complete list of Intelligence Community resources detailing the tradecraft and operations exemplified in this book, along with other bonus content from the authors.

## CENTRAL INTELLIGENCE AGENCY (CIA)
**www.cia.gov**
To learn more about CIA Mission Centers, careers, operations, and tradecraft.

## FEDERAL BUREAU OF INVESTIGATION (FBI)
**www.fbi.gov**
To learn more about FBI careers, operations, surveillance, and tradecraft.

## NATIONAL SECURITY AGENCY (NSA)

**www.nsa.gov**

To learn more about signals intelligence (SIGINT).

## OTHER INTELLIGENCE COMMUNITY (IC) MEMBERS

**www.state.gov**

To learn more about US strategic priorities and surveillance detection.

**www.ignet.gov**

To learn more about the Council of the Inspectors General on Integrity and Efficiency (CIGIE) and the Guidelines on Undercover Operations.

**https://oig.justice.gov**

To learn more about the Office of the Inspector General, the Drug Enforcement Administration (DEA), and its Confidential Source Program.

**www.dni.gov**

To learn more about the Office of the Director of National Intelligence (DNI) and the US National Intelligence and Counterintelligence Strategies.

**www.justice.gov**

To learn more about espionage cases and tradecraft.

**www.ojp.gov**

To learn more about undercover police operations.

# INDEX

# INDEX

# ABOUT THE AUTHORS

**Andrew Bustamante** is a former clandestine CIA intelligence officer and cofounder of EverydaySpy, a one-of-a-kind training platform for adapting the skills of intelligence operatives for business and life. He hosts the *EverydaySpy Podcast,* an iTunes top 100 podcast rated in the top 0.5% of all podcasts worldwide; serves as a go-to expert for international news and security issues; and is a highly sought-after public speaker and respected corporate consultant who has been featured by award-winning news outlets *The Tampa Bay Times* and *Business Insider;* major podcast platforms including *The Diary of a CEO* and *Lex Fridman Podcast,* as well as international TV outlets including FOX, ABC, and the History Channel. A graduate of the United States Air Force Academy and decorated US Air Force combat veteran, he spent the bulk of his military career specializing in nuclear ICBM operations. After winning decorations in both Afghanistan and Iraq, he was recruited into CIA's National Clandestine Service (NCS), where he served for seven years handling sensitive operations still classified Top Secret. Proud parents, Andrew and his wife, Jihi, left CIA to pursue a new mission: building their family and their company.

\* \* \*

# ABOUT THE AUTHORS

**Jihi Bustamante** is a former clandestine CIA targeting officer and co-founder of EverydaySpy. After earning a master of social work and a juris doctor, she was recruited into CIA's National Clandestine Service from a career in social work supporting refugee children and survivors of torture. Unlike her public-facing husband, she remains private in both her personal and professional lives.

# RAISING READERS
## Books Build Bright Futures

hank you for reading this book and for being a reader of books in general. As an uthor, I am so grateful to share being part of a community of readers with you, nd I hope you will join me in passing our love of books on to the next generation readers.

**d you know that reading for enjoyment is the single biggest predictor of a ild's future happiness and success?**

ore than family circumstances, parents' educational background, or income, ading impacts a child's future academic performance, emotional well-being, mmunication skills, economic security, ambition, and happiness.

udies show that kids reading for enjoyment in the US is in rapid decline:

- In 2012, 53% of 9-year-olds read almost every day. Just 10 years later, in 2022, the number had fallen to 39%.
- In 2012, 27% of 13-year-olds read for fun daily. By 2023, that number was just 14%.

Together, we can commit to **Raising Readers** and change this trend. How?

- Read to children in your life daily.
- Model reading as a fun activity.
- Reduce screen time.
- Start a family, school, or community book club.
- Visit bookstores and libraries regularly.
- Listen to audiobooks.
- Read the book before you see the movie.
- Encourage your child to read aloud to a pet or stuffed animal.
- Give books as gifts.
- Donate books to families and communities in need.

BOB1217

**Books build bright futures**, and **Raising Readers** is our shared responsibility.

For more information, visit **JoinRaisingReaders.com**

Sources: National Endowment for the Arts, National Assessment of Educational Progress, WorldBookDay.org, Nielsen BookData's 2023 "Understanding the Children's Book Consumer"